Joseph & Brigham

An Eternal Bond

Cover and interior designed by Sarah Blakely.

ISBN 13: 978-1-952669-09-5

Published by Aspen Books, 226 S. Center St. Santaquin, UT 84655

Library of Congress Control Number: 2021940181

Printed in the United States of America

10 9 8 7 6 5 4 3 2 1

Joseph & Brigham

An Eternal Bond

Susan Easton Black

ASPEN BOOKS

Table of Contents

To early Church members, the sun breaking through clouds symbolized the dawning of the Restoration and the coming of gospel light to illuminate a dark earth. It is little wonder, then, that sunstones were featured prominently on the Nauvoo Temple. Above each sun are two hands holding trumpets, heralding the dawning of the gospel in this dispensation. Parley P. Pratt's hymn "The Morning Breaks" declares:

The morning breaks, the shadows flee;
Lo, Zion's standard is unfurled!
The dawning of a brighter day,
The dawning of a brighter day
Majestic rises on the world.

The clouds of error disappear
Before the rays of truth divine;
The glory bursting from afar,
The glory bursting from afar
Wide o'er the nations soon will shine. [...]

—Angels from heav'n and truth from earth
Have met, and both have record borne;
Thus Zion's light is bursting forth,
Thus Zion's light is bursting forth
To bring her ransomed children home. *

*https://history.churchofjesuschrist.org/content/museum/nauvoo-temple-sunstones

Probable daguerreotype of Joseph Smith by Lucian Foster, April 1844.

Daguerreotype of Brigham Young taken by Marsena Cannon in Salt Lake City in 1853.

Introduction

From his youthful utterances in the Palmyra woods to his manly cry at Carthage, Joseph Smith was the "choice seer" whom the Lord raised up to bring forth the word of God. Revelations, translations, covenants, and eternal truths were the continuum of his life's labor, for he held "the keys of this Last Dispensation, and will forever hold them, both in time and eternity."[1]

Latter-day Saints around the world testify that the Lord Almighty sealed upon Joseph "every Priesthood, every key, every power, every principle that belongs to the last dispensation of the fulness of times, and to the building up of the kingdom of God."[2]
Of the Prophet Joseph, Brigham Young said:

> It was decreed in the councils of eternity, long before the foundations of the earth were laid, that he should be the man, in the last dispensation of this world, to bring forth the word of God to the people, and receive the fulness of the keys and power of the Priesthood of the Son of God.[3]

Joseph Smith's declarations of prophetic revelation resonated with seekers of truth in Western New York. Although contemporaries labeled his followers as ordinary, there was nothing ordinary about their willingness to follow the prophet from New York to Ohio, Missouri, and Illinois. Their holographic writings reveal an unusual capacity for courage and an unflinching faith at a time when religious intolerance raged. Their courage to withstand cruel persecution and encroaching evil and their faith to look to God when all around mocked their convictions is a story of religious commitment. As

1. Lucy Mack Smith History, p. 219. Joseph Smith Papers.

2. Brian H. Stuy, Collected Discourses delivered by Wilford Woodruff, His Two Counselors, the Twelve Apostles and Others 5 vols. (Burbank, CA: B.H.S. Publishing, 1987-1992), 5:317-318.

3. Brigham Young, "Intelligence, etc.," Journal of Discourses 26 vols. (Liverpool: Latter-day Saints' Book Depot, 1858), 7:289.

the world tossed with waves of uncertainty, the strength of the followers of Joseph Smith became a beacon to others searching for eternal truths. For Joseph Smith, he was the man that truth-seekers hoped to meet. William Henry penned:

> You knew he was a true prophet of God because you could not be in his presence without feeling the influence and Spirit of God, which seemed to flow from him almost as heat does from a stove. You could not see it, but you felt it.[4]

4. Callie O. Morley, "History of William and Myra Mayall Henrie, Pioneers of 1847," (Delta, UT: October 1955), p. 4.

Joseph L. Robinson noted:

> The Prophet's voice was like the thunders of heaven, yet his language was meek and his instructions edified much. There was a power and majesty that attended his words and preaching that we never beheld in any man before.[5]

5. Joseph L. Robinson quote, in Hyrum L. Andrus and Helen Mae Andrus, They Knew the Prophet (Salt Lake City: Bookcraft, 1974), p. 64.

Josiah Quincy, a former mayor of Boston, said:

> It is by no means improbable that some future textbook will contain a question something like this: What historical American of the nineteenth century has exerted the most powerful influence upon the destinies of his countrymen? And it is by no means impossible that the answer to the interrogatory may be thus written: Joseph Smith, the Mormon Prophet.[6]

6. Josiah Quincy, Figures of the Past (New York City: Little, Brown, and Co, 1926), p.

Yet noted historians in the United States beg to differ. When considering, who was the American of the nineteenth century that exerted the most powerful influence upon the destinies of his countrymen, many point to

Abraham Lincoln. Those wanting to answer the question in a Latter-day Saint context claim that Joseph Smith was surpassed in influence by his successor Brigham Young. After all, few leaders of the nineteenth century match the dogged determination of Brigham.

From humble beginnings in an obscure village in Vermont, Brigham rose to the applause of thinking men, but more importantly, he grew in favor with God. Although most would contend that the arduous toil of farm labor and unwelcome poverty dominated his early years, it was his unwavering search for eternal truth that permeated his thoughts. Reading the Book of Mormon, listening to missionaries, and being baptized brought answers to his search. Brigham said:

> When I saw a man without eloquence, or talents for public speaking, who could only say, 'I know, by the power of the Holy Ghost, that the Book of Mormon is true, that Joseph Smith is a Prophet of the Lord,' the Holy Ghost proceeding from that individual illuminated my understanding, and light, glory, and immortality were before me.[7]

7. Brigham Young, "March of Mormonism—The Power of God and the Wisdom of Man—Good and Evil Influences—The Law of Increase," Journal of Discourses, 1:91.

Brigham stood by the Prophet Joseph Smith in the best and worst of times and claimed to know the prophet better than anyone. Brigham never saw himself stepping above Joseph. He saw his role as defending him at every turn. One evening in Kirtland, Brigham overheard a man loudly rail against Joseph Smith, saying, "Woe! woe! unto the inhabitants of this place." Brigham reacted:

> [I] put my pants and shoes on, took my cowhide, went out, and laying hold of him, jerked him round, and assured him that if he did not stop his noise and

> let the people enjoy their sleep without interruption, I would cowhide him on the spot, for we had the Lord's Prophet right here, and we did not want the Devil's prophet yelling round the streets.[8]

8. Elden Jay Watson, comp., Brigham Young: A Chronology of Known Addresses of the Prophet Brigham Young (Salt Lake City: E. Watson, 1979), pp. 17-18.

Following the assassination of Joseph Smith at Carthage Jail, Brigham determined to carry forward the mighty work started by his beloved prophet. He encouraged the completion of the Nauvoo Temple by saying:

> We want to build the Temple in this place, if we have to build it as the Jews built the walls of the Temple in Jerusalem, with a sword in one hand and the trowel in the other.[9]

9.Journal History of the Church, August 18, 1844.

Under Brigham's direction the temple was built and the Saints were endowed before the great exodus from Nauvoo. The Saints moved west and settled in small communities throughout the Intermountain West. They were willing to defend their settlements against the US Army. Brigham's fame by the 1860s was so widespread that when war cries threatened to divide the nation along the Mason-Dixon Line, President Abraham Lincoln said, "You tell Brigham Young if he will leave me alone, I'll leave him alone."[10] Even the most skeptical historian is forced to concede that Brigham was a man with a mission and a vision.

10. Abraham Lincoln quote, in Leonard J. Arrington, Brigham Young, American Moses (NY: Alfred A. Knopf, 1985), p. 195.

Naturally, questions have arisen concerning the relationship between Joseph Smith and Brigham Young, two leaders called of God to fulfill a marvelous work. Some historians view Joseph Smith as an inspired, visionary prophet and Brigham Young as his disciple—the practical doer who executed Joseph's plans. Others depict Brigham Young as a resolute administrator and powerful leader of men who made workable the visions of Joseph.

The purpose of this work is to clearly show the relationship between Joseph Smith and Brigham Young—two men bound together in the cause of Christ. Read of these stalwart men who looked heavenward for answers and sacrificed life's comforts for eternal truths. Theirs is a story of friendship, loyalty, and unwavering testimony of the Restoration. Joseph and Brigham were different in stature, talents, and demeanor, but when it came to defending the truth, they were one. Yet there were rough patches along their journey.

Brigham endured chastisement from Joseph when gratitude may have been more appropriate. Even at these times, Brigham never lost confidence in Joseph's prophetic calling.

Theirs is a story that may never be fully known, but must be told for it reveals a story of friendship based on the gospel of Jesus Christ.

Stained glass window created in 1913
for the Adams Ward chapel in
Los Angeles, CA.

Chapter One
The Early Years

Joseph Smith

By 1805 economic shenanigans of unscrupulous men had left Father Smith with few options and little hope. Poverty is never a welcomed guest. Its accompanying ills may have given Mother Smith pause as she anticipated delivering yet another child. In announcing the birth of her newborn, she merely penned, "In the meantime we had a son, whom we called Joseph after the name of his father."[11] Thus, without fanfare on the wintry day of December 23, 1805 in Sharon, Vermont, Joseph Smith Jr. was born.

11. Lucy Mack Smith, History, 1845, p. 51. Joseph Smith Papers.

His earliest years consisted of typical frontier activities for the age—exploring his environs and dwelling in log cabins. His father tried his best to make ends meet by cultivating farms on rocky soil and teaching school in the winter months. Some years he found success making a living as a farmer and a school teacher; others he did not. After a time and "in this way . . . our circumstances gradually improved," wrote Mother Smith.

By 1811 yesteryear's woes had passed, but "this state of things did not long continue."[12] A hopeful move to West Lebanon, New Hampshire proved an intense crucible for the Smiths. Typhus fever, an illness that had caused six thousand deaths in the Connecticut Valley, did not spare the Smith household. Young Joseph endured his two-week bout with fever only to find this was the beginning of a struggle that would mar his childhood.

12. Ibid., p. 56.

13. Lucy Mack Smith, History, 1844-1845, Page [1], bk. 3. Joseph Smith Papers.

When Father Smith learned that his son had consented to an operation, he cast "his eyes upon his boy . . . [and] burst into a flood of tears."[13] Although the procedure relieved pain and removed a diseased portion of the bone in his leg, 14 additional pieces of bone worked their way out of the incision before healing. During these difficult days, Uncle Jesse Smith agreed to care for young Joseph in his home off the coast of Massachusetts. Sea breezes and constant care helped Joseph's health stabilize. He then rejoined his family who were still facing poverty.

14. Lucy Mack Smith, History, 1845, p. 63

"We were compelled to strain every energy to provide for our present necessities, instead of making arrangements for the future," wrote Mother Smith.[14] Hoping better land in the state of Vermont would provide needed economic relief, the Smiths moved onto rural

Norwich. Father Smith tilled the soil but without success. "The first year our crops failed; . . . The crops the second year were as the year before—a perfect failure. . . . The next year an untimely frost destroyed the crops." Discouraged, Mother Smith wrote, "This was enough."[15]

15. Ibid., p. 65.

In 1816 Father Smith ventured from Vermont to Palmyra, New York where stately trees, the proposed Erie Canal, and cheap prices for virgin farmland held the promise of a brighter future. He employed opportunist Caleb Howard to transport Mother Smith and their children to the western climes of Palmyra. En route to what would become the "Cradle of the Restoration,"

16. Ibid., p. 67.

Howard proved himself "an unprincipled and unfeeling wretch." He forced young Joseph "to travel miles at a time on foot, notwithstanding he was still lame."[16] Joseph stated, "I suffered the most excruciating weariness & pain [at his hands and was]... left to wallow in my blood." Joseph was able to make the long journey due to the kindness of a stranger who "picked me up, & carried me to the Town" of Palmyra.[17]

17. History, 1838-1856, volume A-1 [23 December 1805-30 August 1834], p. 132. Joseph Smith Papers.

Hoping to put behind them what was becoming an alarming economic situation, members of the Smith household looked for ways to improve the family's finances. Father Smith opened a small bakeshop on Main Street, offering customers gingerbread, pies, and root beer. Mother Smith used her artistic talents to paint oilcloth coverings. Joseph's siblings found jobs as common laborers rocking up wells and working as farmhands.

The Smiths' hard work paid off. In 1818 they had saved enough to contract for a hundred-acre farm. The farm was in a beautiful wooded tract about two miles south of the Palmyra village. From the beginning, the mortgaged farm venture was successful. "I believe something like thirty acres of land were got ready for cultivation the first year," wrote Mother Smith.

By the second year she boasted, "We had a snug log house, neatly furnished, and the means of living comfortably."[18] Within two years, the Smiths had turned their wooded acreage into a productive farm. On the heels of their success came a sense of belonging and a sense of permanence. Mother Smith wrote:

18. Lucy Mack Smith, History, 1844-1845, page [6], bk. 3.

> If we might judge by external manifestations, we had every reason to believe that we had many good and affectionate friends for never have I seen more kindness or attention shown to any person or family than we received from those around us.[19]

19. Ibid., p. 8.

In early spring of 1820, cordial neighbors turned from friend to foe. It wasn't any untoward action of Father or Mother Smith that caused the alienation. A curious message told to an itinerant minister by 14-year-old

Joseph Smith Jr. caused townsfolk to withdraw fellowship. Youthful Joseph told the preacher that he had seen a heavenly vision on his family farm. Oddly enough, the mere mention of this truth sparked a flame of Smith hatred that went unchecked in Palmyra for years. The teenager's unwavering affirmation that God the Father and his Son Jesus Christ appeared to him in the Palmyra woods did not help the damaged social situation of the Smiths.

Even though men in high standing in town boasted of heavenly raptures of their own, it was the grandiose account of Joseph's First Vision that angered the community. Community leaders wanted only confessing, if not contending Christians living in their town. They wanted a community of upstanding citizens who shouted praises to God. A young boy claiming to know better than they had no place in their town. "Priest contending against priest, and convert against convert" was acceptable, but not the challenging views of young Joseph Smith (JS-History 1:6).

It is remarkable that under such severe pressure from so many, Joseph refused to veer from proclaiming that he had seen,

> a pillar of light exactly over my head, above the brightness of the sun, which descended gradually until it fell upon me.... When the light rested upon me I saw two Personages, whose brightness and glory defy all description, standing above me in the air. One of them spake unto me, calling me by name and said, pointing to the other—This is My Beloved Son. Hear Him!" Jesus Christ told Joseph that he must not unite himself with any denomination for "all their creeds were an abomination in his sight; that those professors were all corrupt.(JS-History 1:17, 19)

The divine answer was clear to young Joseph but not to townsfolk. They tried to convince him that his vision was "all of the devil, that there were no such things as visions or revelations in these days; that all such things had ceased with the apostles" (JS-History 1:21). Then, as if to censor the boy for his resolute stance, ministers and farmers withdrew from him and cast aspersions upon not only the teenager but the Smith family. Joseph said:

> Though I was an obscure boy, only between fourteen and fifteen years of age, and my circumstances in life such as to make a boy of no consequence in the world, yet men of high standing would take notice sufficient to excite the public mind against me, and create a bitter persecution.

In the wake of persecution came ostracism and personal sorrow to Joseph and his family. Yet nothing could make the boy deny that he had seen Divine Beings in the woods on his family farm.

> I had actually seen a light, and in the midst of that light I saw two Personages, and they did in reality speak to me; and though I was hated and persecuted for saying that I had seen a vision, yet it was true; . . . I knew it, and I knew that God knew it, and I could not deny it. (JS-History 1:22, 25)

Epithets such as "lazy," "illiterate," "superstitious," "disorderly," "a drunkard," "an imposter," and "addicted to vice and the grossest immoralities" were hurled at the young boy.[20] When farmer Thomas Taylor was asked, "Why didn't they like [young Joseph]?" He answered, "To tell the truth, there was something about him they

20. Eber D. Howe, Mormonism Unvailed (Painesville, OH: E. D. Howe, 1834), pp. 249, 259.

could not understand; some way he knew more than they did, and it made them mad."[21] Townsfolk became so upset by Joseph and his vision that they refused to hire any Smiths for even a menial chore. "We never knew we were bad folks until Joseph told his vision," penned Joseph's youngest brother William. "We were considered respectable till then, but at once people began to circulate falsehoods and stories."[22]

One churchgoing man said:

> The very influence the boy carried was the danger they feared for the coming generation, that not only the young men, but all who came in contact with him, would follow him and he must be put down.[23]

The mob-like tone of his sentiment was followed by untoward actions that caused young Joseph and his family to fear.

A greater fear for Joseph, however, was introspective thoughts about his behavior: "I frequently fell into many foolish errors, and displayed the weakness of youth, and the foibles of human nature" (JS-History 1:28). Yet he confessed, "I have not, neither can it be sustained, in truth, been guilty of wronging or injuring any man or society of men."[24] But for a boy who had talked with Heavenly Beings face to face and had suffered "severe persecution at the hands of all classes of men, both religious and irreligious, because I continued to affirm that I had seen a vision," his behavior caused self-condemnation. (JS-History 1:27, 29)

Brigham Young

Brigham was the ninth of eleven children born to farmer and Revolutionary War veteran, John Young and his

21. Juvenile Instructor 17 (October 1, 1882), p. 302.

22. Deseret Evening News, January 20, 1894.

23. "Stories from the Notebook of Martha Cox, Grandmother of Fern Cox Anderson," in Ivan J. Barrett, Young Joseph (Salt Lake City: RIC Publishing, Inc., 1981), p. 54.

24. Letter of Joseph Smith to Oliver Cowdery, December 1834. Joseph Smith Papers.

wife Abigail Howe. Brigham was born June 1, 1801 in Whitingham, Vermont, four years before Joseph Smith. Before his third birthday and after four moves in the Whitingham area, Brigham's family located 135 miles southwest in the Finger Lakes region of Central New York, the hilly countryside of Sherburne. At the time, the town of Sherburne didn't have so much as a decent road or a marketplace, but it had rich soil that promised a bountiful harvest.

At an early age, Brigham worked alongside his father and his brothers to clear, plow, and plant the family farm. Of his labors Brigham said:

> At an early age I labored with my father, assisting him to clear off new land and cultivate his farm, passing through many hardships and privations incident to settling a new country.[25]

25. Watson, Manuscript History of Brigham Young, p. 1.

Due to the hours required to labor on the farm, Brigham spent little time learning to read and write. He claimed to have only spent eleven days in a formal school setting. Of his youth Brigham remarked:

> We had the privilege of picking up brush, chopping down trees, rolling logs, and working amongst the roots, and of getting our shins, feet, and toes bruised. . . . I learned to make bread, wash the dishes, milk the cows, and can make butter; and can beat most of the women in this community at housekeeping. Those are about all the advantages I gained in my youth. I know how to economi[z]e, for my father had to do it.[26]

26. Brigham Young, "Joseph Smith's family—Bashfulness in Public Speaking—the Coming Crisis—Counsel," Journal of Discourses, 5:97.

The bottom line as Brigham recalled his early years and the years that followed: "I have been a poor boy and a poor man, and my parents were poor."[27]

Brigham was so lacking in the expected necessities to sustain life that he often went to bed hungry and just as often got out of bed to eat slices of buttered bread. Perhaps that is why in later years, when he had a family of his own, "cupboards were full of crackers, fruit, and molasses so that his children need not be hungry between meals."[28]

Under such impoverished circumstances, physical work of even the youngest child was expected. Winters were spent clearing trees and brush off the land so crops could be planted in the spring. Summers were spent weeding and watering so that when autumn came, crops could be harvested and sold to the highest bidder. Profits made from the harvests were used to pay down the mortgage on the farm. And so it went year after year, unless crops failed leaving the mortgage unpaid. For the Young family, crop failures led to more than one move in New York.

To help his father make ends meet, Brigham was hired out to near neighbors when his chores were done. Of his early employment, he said:

> I have believed all my life that that which was worth doing was worth doing well, and have considered it as much a part of my religion to do honest, reliable works, such as would endure, for those who employed me.[29]

With such an honest attitude, employment opportunities came readily to Brigham. Neighbors used such words such as "upright" and "sober" to describe his work ethic.

As a youth Brigham was aware of his reputation and sought in language and in deed to conduct himself "in

27. Brigham Young, "The Power and Importance of Economy—Domestic Extravagance and Mismanagement, with Their Bad Results," Journal of Discourses, 4:312.

28. Linda Cory Hardy, Boys Who Became Prophets (Salt Lake City: Deseret Book, 1982), p. 10.

29. Brigham Young to George Hickox, 19 February 1876. Brigham Young Papers. Church History Library, Salt Lake City.

a way to gain for myself the respect of the moral and good among my neighbors."[30] He said, "I do not know that I ever wronged my neighbor, even to the value of a pin."[31] He added, "I have not infringed upon any law, or trod upon the rights of my neighbors."[32] Even though money was tight in his family, Brigham claimed that he never "stole, lied, gambled, got drunk, or disobeyed my parents."[33] He summed up his youth by saying, "I have tried to walk in the paths of righteousness."[34]

Brigham's desire to walk in righteousness was nurtured and cultivated in his parental home. His parents, John and Abigail Young, gave their children strict religious and moral instructions. Brigham said of his parents:

> [They were] some of the most strict religionists that lived upon the earth. . . . When I was young, I was kept within very strict bounds, and was not allowed to walk more than half-an-hour on Sunday for exercise. The proper and necessary gambols of youth [were] denied me. . . . I had not a chance to dance when I was young, and never heard the enchanting tones of the violin, until I was eleven years of age; and then I thought I was on the high way to hell, if I suffered myself to linger and listen to it.[35]

Brigham's upbringing was so strict that if he exclaimed "Devil," he had sworn "very wickedly." His father reacted to such words with "a word and a blow . . . but the blow came first."[36]

Not wanting to repeat such a strict upbringing with his own children, Brigham wrote, "I shall not subject my little children to such a course of unnatural training, but they shall go to the dance, study music, read novels, and do anything else that will tend to expand their frames,

30. Brigham Young, "Temporal and Spiritual Duties of the Saints—Benefits Resulting from Proper Parental Authority—Connection Betwixt Temporal and Spiritual Things—Character of Joseph the Prophet,—All Blessings from the Lord," Journal of Discourses, 10:360.

31. Brigham Young, "Extensive Character of the Gospel.—Comprehensiveness of Divine Revelations, etc." Journal of Discourses, 6:290.

32. Brigham Young "Knowledge of the Doctrine of Christ—The Religions of Men, and the Religion of God—Joseph Smith—Persecutions, etc.," Journal of Discourses, 1:41

33. Brigham Young, "Personal Reminiscences, etc.," Journal of Discourses, 8:38.

34. Brigham Young "Knowledge of the Doctrine of Christ—The Religions of Men, and the Religion of God—Joseph Smith—Persecutions, etc.," Journal of Discourses, 1:41.

35. Brigham Young, "Extensive Character of the Gospel.—Comprehensiveness of Divine Revelations, etc.," Journal of Discourses 6:290; Brigham Young, "Organization and Development of Man," Journal of Discourses, 2:94.

36. Brigham Young, "Extensive Character of the Gospel.—Comprehensiveness of Divine Revelations, etc." Journal of Discourses, 6:290; Brigham Young, "Discord at Meetings Rebuked—A Text for Speakers at the Conference—Subject for the People—A Call for Mules, Horses, Wagons, Teamsters, Flour, etc.," Journal of Discourses, 4:112.

add fire to their spirits, improve their minds, and make them feel free and untrammeled in body and mind."[37]

Yet Brigham did not reject religion based on his parents' application. It would be difficult to do so being raised in the Young household and in the hotbed of religious excitement in New York. Brigham wrote:

> Priests had urged me to pray before I was eight years old. On this subject I had but one prevailing feeling in my mind—Lord, preserve me until I am old enough to have sound judgment, and a discreet mind ripened upon a good solid foundation of common sense.[38]

Throughout his youth, Brigham heard priests and pastors alike cry, "'Lo here is Christ, lo there is Christ,' ... each claiming that it had the Savior, and that others were wrong.[39]

Being an observer, Brigham witnessed Methodist camp meetings and revival scenes in New York. "I had seen men and women fall, and be as speechless and breathless as that stove before me," he later recalled, claiming such actions were "what they called the power of God."[40] He also saw,

> Them get religion all around me—men were rolling and hollering and bawling and thumping but it had no effect on me—I wanted to know the truth that I might not be fooled—children and young men got religion, but I could not.[41]

Brigham listened to famed Methodist preacher Lorenzo Dow speak in hopes of catching the spirit and perhaps fitting in with his neighbors. Yet he wrote:

37. Brigham Young, "Organization and Development of Man," Journal of Discourses, 2:94.

38. Brigham Young, "Personal Reminiscences, etc.," Journal of Discourses, 8:37.

39. Brigham Young, "Good and Evil—The Testimony of the Spirit—His Early Religious Experience," Journal of Discourses, 14:112.

40. Brigham Young, "Secret of Happiness—Self Examination—Joseph Smith a Man of Obedience to God—Baptism for the Dead—Temporal and Spiritual One—a Dream—Order of Enoch, the Order of God—A Good Word for the Women," Journal of Discourses, 18:247.

41. Minutes, 8 January 1845. Brigham Young Papers. Church History Library.

> [Lorenzo Dow] stood up some of the time and he sat down some of the time; he was in this position and in that position, and talked two or three hours, and when he got through I asked myself "What have you learned from Lorenzo Dow?" and my answer was, nothing but morals. He could tell the people they should not work on the Sabbath day; they should not lie, swear, steal, commit adultery, etc., but when he came to teaching the things of God, he was as dark as midnight.[42]

42. Hardy, Boys Who Became Prophets, p. 11.

Perhaps it was his disappointment with the preaching of Lorenzo Dow or the sights and sounds of the camp meetings that led Brigham on a quest, a self-appointed search to find a satisfying religion and "the path that leads to the kingdom of heaven."[43] His quest was in earnest and led him to attend a variety of religious meetings. Brigham said:

43. Brigham Young, "Salvation the Result of Individual Exertion," Journal of Discourses, 9:248.

> I used to go to meetings—was well acquainted with the Episcopalians, Presbyterians, New Lights, Baptists, Freewill Baptists, Wesleyan and Reformed Methodists,—lived from my youth where I was acquainted with Quakers as well as the other denominations, and was more or less acquainted with almost every other religious ism... I understood the Scriptures tolerably well, and my whole mind and reflections were to seek for every particle of truth with regard to doctrine. I always admired morality, and never saw a day in which I did not respect a good, moral, sensible man far more than I could respect a wicked man.[44]

44. Brigham Young, "Personal Reminiscences, etc.," Journal of Discourses, 8:38.

As to finding a religion that satisfied him, Brigham came up short. Preachers and their followers noticed young Brigham and taunted him for not joining with a faith group. Brigham said:

> I was called an infidel because I could not embrace their dogmas... There were some things they preached I could believe, and some I could not... As far as their teachings were in accordance with the Bible, I could believe them, and no further.[45]

45. Brigham Young, "Secret of Happiness—Self Examination—Joseph Smith a Man of Obedience to God—Baptism for the Dead—Temporal and Spiritual One—a Dream—Order of Enoch, the Order of God—A Good Word for the Women," Journal of Discourses, 18:247.

Brigham believed in the existence of a God that had created the sun, moon, and stars. As he listened to those who professed a particular religion, he was unsettled by their ungodly talk and unchristian acts.

> He overheard a minster's wife say to another woman, 'Do you suppose that we shall be under the necessity of eating with our hired help when we get into heaven? We do not do it here, and I have an idea that there will be two tables in heaven.' He saw supposedly good, honest men take advantage of their neighbors and oppress and cheat them.[46]

46. Hardy, Boys Who Became Prophets, p. 11.

He said, "I wanted no religion that produced such morals."[47] Reading the Bible convinced him that the true religion must be more than good morals. There must be authority and structure such as existed at the time of Christ and His Apostles. Brigham said:

47. Ibid.

> I understood from the Bible that when the Lord had a church upon the earth it was a system of ordinances, of laws and regulations to be obeyed, a society presided over and regulated by officers and ministers peculiar to itself to answer such and such purposes, and to bring to pass such and such results.[48]

48. Brigham Young, "The Kingdom of God on Earth is a Living, Moving, Effective Institution: We Do not Carry It, But It Carries Us," Journal of Discourses, 11:254.

As Brigham grew older, he grew bolder. He questioned ministers and wanted to know "how the kingdom of God should be built up if the New Testament pattern was not the way." He was answered, "'My dear friend these things are done away with.' Ordinances? Mere matters of ceremony; belief was sufficient." With answers insufficient, Brigham reached the inescapable conclusion, "I knew that Jesus Christ had no true Church upon the earth."[49] At the same time Brigham believed that,

> he would gladly give all the gold and silver he ever could possess to meet with one individual who could show me anything about God, heaven, or the plan of salvation. [50]

It was in the days of his youth that he longed to see a prophet. Brigham wrote:

> I felt in those days, that if I could see the face of a prophet, such as had lived on the earth in former times, a man that had revelations, to whom the heavens were opened, who knew God and his character, I would freely circumscribe the earth on my hands and knees; I thought that there was no hardship but what I would undergo, if I could see one person that knew what God is and where he is, what was his character, and what eternity was.[51]

His longings were encouraged by his mother Abigail Young who was a "praying, fervent" woman.[52]

She taught Brigham and his siblings "to honour the name of the Father and the Son, and to reverence the [Bible]."

49. Brigham Young, "The Kingdom of God on Earth is a Living, Moving, Effective Institution: We Do not Carry It, But It Carries Us," Journal of Discourses, 11:254.

50. Brigham Young, "Salvation the Result of Individual Exertion," Journal of Discourses, 9:248.

51. Deseret News Weekly, October 8, 1856.

52. S. Dilworth Young, Here is Brigham... Brigham Young... the years to 1844 (Salt Lake City: Bookcraft, 1964), p. 32.

She often said of the Holy Bible:

> Read it, observe its precepts, and apply them to your lives as far as you can; do everything that is good; do nothing that is evil; and if you see any persons in distress, administer to their wants. . . . Don't ever become angry for if you do, you'll be overcome by evil.[53]

53. Hardy, Boys Who Became Prophets, p. 13.

Brigham loved his mother and heeded her words as if they were her last. It is little wonder that he listened to her words so attentively, for she struggled with the dreaded illness of tuberculosis for years. He recalled the day his father rushed out of their home to the fields to bring him back to the house. When Brigham arrived at their cabin, he found his mother had died from tuberculosis complications. His hardest years followed her death. Biographer Ronald K. Esplin wrote:

> Without mother keeping house, the older children moved on, and the family was divided. Brigham and younger brother Lorenzo accompanied their father, breaking land for a new farm and harvesting sugar maple on isolated acreage near the southern tip of Seneca Lake. During this difficult period they barely had enough to eat.[54]

54. Ronald K. Esplin, "Conversion and Transformation: Brigham Young's New York Roots and the Search for Bible Religion," in Larry C. Porter, Milton V. Backman Jr., and Susan Easton Black, eds. Regional Studies in Latter-day Saint History: New York (Provo, UT: Department of Church History and Doctrine, Brigham Young University, 1992), p. 166.

Brigham's younger brother Lorenzo recalled that he and Brigham "were left alone for a few days while their father went for food, they began growing faint from living only on the insubstantial maple sugar." Yet the Lord was ever mindful of them. One example of the Lord's mindfulness occurred when Brigham was fifteen years old. His brother Lorenzo had a vivid dream in which he saw a magnificent gold carriage being drawn by a pair of white horses. Lorenzo wrote:

> It was manifested to me that the Savior was in the carriage, and that it was driven by His servant. It stopped near me and the Savior inquired, "Where is your Brother Brigham?" After answering His question He inquired about my other brothers, and concerning my father... He stated that He wanted us all, but especially my brother Brigham.[55]

55. James A. Little, "Biography of Lorenzo Dow Young," Utah Historical Quarterly (1946), 14:26.

The interpretation or understanding of the dream would not be known for years. One year after the dream Brigham recalled, "When I was 16 years of age, my father said to me, 'You can now have your time; go and provide for yourself.'" With the reality of providing for himself, Brigham "stopped running, jumping, wrestling and the laying out of my strength for naught."[56] He moved from his father's home to Auburn, New York, in the picturesque Finger Lakes region known for its theological seminary. Brigham resided with relatives for a time while apprenticed to John C. Jeffries, a chairmaker and a housepainter.

56. Brigham Young, "Temporal and Spiritual Duties of the Saints—Benefits Resulting from Proper Parental Authority—Connection Betwixt Temporal and Spiritual Things—Character of Joseph the Prophet—All Blessings from the Lord," Journal of Discourses, 10:360.

By age 18 Brigham had learned his craft well. He moved to Aurelius, New York, a small town that borders Auburn on the east. He set up a woodworking shop and in so doing, became the town carpenter, joiner, painter, and glazier. As for farming, a trade that had occupied his childhood and youth, he was still a farmer. Everyone farmed. But his greater interest was in his vocation.

Two Young Men

As a matter of summation, Joseph Smith and Brigham Young, who would later become the closest of friends in the cause of Christ, had their early beginnings in the state of Vermont before moving to New York. During their youth, they both wanted to know eternal truths and attended worship services in hopes of finding a religion that satisfied their longings.

For Joseph, his answer came in a vision of God the Father and His Son Jesus Christ. For Brigham, his quest for religious truth went unanswered. Both experienced persecution from townsfolk—Joseph for not denying the truths he had learned from Heaven and Brigham for not joining with one faith or another.

Although the young boys had similar religious leanings and an upbringing of farm labor and poverty, there was never the chance meeting. There was never a time when Brigham or Joseph were together at a revival camp meeting in New York or in the same place selling produce from a harvest. That day would come, but not until Brigham and Joseph had become men.

Brigham Young and his brothers. Taken 13 September 1866 by C. R. Savage. They are from left to right, youngest to oldest, Lorenzo Dow Young, Brigham Young, Phineas Howe Young, Joseph Young, and John Young Jr.

Chapter Two

Preparing the Way

Brigham Young supported himself as a painter, carpenter, and glazier for six years before his marriage on October 8, 1824 to Miriam Works. A neighbor described Miriam as a "beautiful blond with blue eyes and wavy hair; gentle and lovable," and Brigham as "vigorous, handsome and magnetic . . . as fine a specimen of young manhood as I have ever known."[57]

57. Mary Van Sickle Wait, Brigham Young in Cayuga County, 1813-1829 (Ithaca, NY: DeWitt Historical Society, 1964), p. 39.

Twenty-three-year-old Brigham and his 18-year-old bride Miriam established their home in Haydenville, north of Auburn, New York (about 40 miles east of Palmyra). In that small agrarian community, Brigham was recognized as a fine artisan and craftsman and is remembered for his skills in creating beautiful "stairwell decorations, fanlight doorways, door frames, stair rails, louvered attic windows and, above all—fireplace mantels."[58] His daughter Susa Young Gates later gave a more laudatory description of Brigham's woodworking skills: "He excelled when the interiors were planned and finished, with a keen feeling for minor decorations of a chaste and substantial nature... He had that care for detail, that appreciation for form and proportion that gave the classic touch to simple models. His mantels, fireplaces, doorways, and cupboards are worthy of the study of trained architects today."[59]

58. Ibid., p. 24.

59. Ibid., p. 41.

After a few short months in Haydenville, Brigham and Miriam located in Port Byron, New York, a thriving city about ten miles north of Haydenville on the banks of the Erie Canal. Possibilities for advancement in Brigham's trade were good in Port Byron, for the canal made it possible to send his woodworking products beyond the region along the Erie Canal to prospective buyers in the east.

The Youngs were residing in a small rented frame house when they welcomed Elizabeth, the first of their two daughters into their home. Brigham supported his family by farming in the summer months and by pursuing his crafts in the winter. To supplement his income, he found regular employment at a cording mill and a paint factory. He had little time for recreation.

While working in the paint factory, Brigham invented a water-powered pigment crusher to reduce the pigment when mixing powder with oil and lead. The crusher device was simple in design yet considered ingenious in his day. He used an old cannon ball as the pestle to an iron pot mortar. The device saved him a great deal of work in mixing paints and provided value to his employer.[60] His work at the paint factory went well until his employer asked him to adulterate or change the quality of the linseed oil in the paint mixes like his competitors. Brigham later wrote, "I had either to be dishonest or quit; and I quit."[61]

Brigham not only quit his work, he quit Port Byron. He packed up his possessions and moved his family north to Oswego, a port city located on the banks of Lake Ontario. In this picturesque setting, Brigham went into business for himself and supported his family "by making and repairing chairs, tables, and cupboards and installing windows, doors, stairways, and fireplace mantels."[62] Brigham succeeded on all fronts—he had a beautiful wife, a growing family, and more calls for work than he could fulfill.

If it wasn't for an insatiable yearning for answers to

60. See Young, Here is Brigham... p. 41.

61. Brigham Young, "True Testimony, Prepare for Coming Events, Corruption of the Government, Etc.," Journal of Discourses, 9:29.

62. Teachings of Presidents of the Church: Brigham Young (Salt Lake City: The Church of Jesus Christ of Latter-day Saints, 1997), p. 2.

religious questions, his life would have felt complete. Hoping to resolve his religious uncertainties, he and his wife Miriam joined the Reformed Methodist Church in Oswego, with Brigham insisting on baptism by immersion. (The Reformed Methodists accepted a variety of baptisms, believing the ordinance more important than the means of baptism). Brigham's affiliation with Methodism was brief. He preferred worshipping with "seekers" in a loosely organized society than with neighbors listening to a minister. With fellow seekers, Brigham could pray, sing, and praise God.

In the fall of 1827 in Oswego, Brigham and his wife Miriam saw a remarkable vision in the sky. Brigham said, "I gazed at it with my Wife—the light was perfectly clear and remained several hours—it formed into men like as if there were great armies."[63] In Mendon, New York, the same vision was seen by his father John Young, his sister Rhoda, his brother-in-law John P. Greene, Heber C. Kimball, and others. Details of the vision were given by Heber C. Kimball:

63. "Synopsis of the History of Heber Chase Kimball," Deseret News, March 31, 1858-April 28, 1858.

> ...it was so clear that you could see to pick up a pin, we looked to the eastern horizon and beheld a white smoke arise towards the heavens, and as it ascended it formed itself into a belt, and made a noise like the rushing of a mighty wind, and continued southwest, forming a regular bow dipping in the western horizon. After the bow had formed it began to widen out and grow clear and transparent of a blueish cast, it grew wide enough to contain twelve men abreast.
>
> In this bow an army moved, commencing from the east and marching to the west. They moved in platoons, and walked so close, the rear ranks trod in the steps of their file leaders, until the whole bow

> was literally crowded with soldiers. We could see distinctly the muskets, bayonets, and knapsacks of the men, who wore caps and feathers like those used by the American soldiers in the last war with Britain; also their officers with their swords and equipage, and heard the clashing and jingling of their instruments of war and could discover the form and features of the men.
>
> The most profound order existed throughout the entire army, when the foremost man stepped, every man stepped at the same time: I could hear the step. When the front rank reached the Western horizon a battle ensued, as we could distinctly hear the report of the arms and the rush. . . . This scenery we gazed upon for hours until it began to disappear.[64]

64. Young, Here is Brigham..., pp. 46-47.

Heber C. Kimball also wrote, "My wife, Vilate, being frightened at what she saw, said, 'Father Young, what does all this mean?' He replied in a lively, pleased manner, 'Why, it's one of the signs of the coming of the Son of Man.'"[65]

65. Young, Here is Brigham..., pp. 46-47.

Mendon, New York

In 1829 Brigham and Miriam moved once again, the fourth move in five years of marriage. This time, the move was to Mendon, New York. It was not the land or employment opportunities in Mendon that caused Brigham and his wife to pack up their belongings and move again; it was family. Brigham's father John Young and sisters Fanny, Mariah, and Rhoda and their families were residing in Mendon.

His brothers Lorenzo and Phinehas lived nearby. These family members were seekers after religious truths, much like Brigham. A few had seen the open vision in the sky in the fall of 1827. Others, like his brother Phinehas, were preachers associated with mainstream churches in the area.

With a large family contingency in the greater Mendon area and with family members sharing similar views about Christianity, it seemed only right that Brigham and Miriam would resettle in Mendon. They put down roots in a town that was becoming an affluent suburb of Rochester. On his father's farm, Brigham built a small home and a woodworking shop next to a stream which allowed him to use a waterwheel to power his mill machinery. His future looked bright.

As Brigham and Miriam settled into their home and became part of the fabric of Mendon society, they made close friends in town. One especially close relationship was with Brigham's cousin, Heber C. Kimball, an accomplished potter by trade. Brigham and Heber shared similar feelings about excellence in their crafts and their quest for religious truth.

Although this should have been a time of joy, being surrounded by loved ones and having more than a modicum of success with his woodworking skills, Brigham knew much of gloominess and despair. Perhaps it had something to do with his frequent moves from town to town. Perhaps it had more to do with satisfying his spiritual longings. His gloominess was not new, just more difficult to handle. Brigham wrote in his journal:

> There was more or less of a gloom over my feelings from the earliest days of my childhood that I have in any recollection. Before I possessed the spirit of the Gospel, I was troubled with that which I heard others complain of, that is, with, at times, feeling cast down, gloomy and desponding, with everything

wearing to me, at times, a dreary aspect. They appeared at times as though a veil was brooding over them, which cast a dark shade upon all things, like the shade of the valley of death, and I felt lonesome and bad.[66]

66. Hardy, Boys Who Became Prophets, p. 14.

According to his biographer Ronald K. Esplin, Brigham was not alone in feeling cast down. His friend Heber recalled,

> ... feeling so gloomy during his period that he wished he were dead. Brigham's brothers Joseph and Phinehas sometimes expressed the same heaviness. According to Phinehas, both he and Brigham felt so disheartened in the fall of 1829 that they could not even pray with any enthusiasm. At the time Phinehas, echoing a common primitivism hope, tried to encourage his brother that surely things would soon change: 'Hang on,' he said, 'for I know the Lord is agoing to do some thing for us.'[67]

67. Ronald K. Esplin, "Conversion and Transformation: Brigham Young's New York Routes and the Search for Bible Religion," pp. 177-178; See Heber Kimball, 8 January 1845. Brigham Young Papers; Phinehas Young to Brigham Young, 11 August 1845, Brigham Young Papers.

The Lord Prepared the Way

The Lord had already begun to prepare a way that would ease the gloominess of the Young family and their friends. On the evening of September 21, 1823, 17-year-old Joseph Smith pled "for forgiveness of all my sins and follies, and also for a manifestation to me, that I might know of my state and standing before him."

While praying, "I discovered a light appearing in my room, which continued to increase until the room was lighter than at noonday, when immediately a personage appeared at my bedside, standing in the air, for his feet did not touch the floor." The angelic personage "called me by name, and said unto me that he was a messenger sent from the presence of God to me, and that his name was Moroni" (JS-History 1:29-30, 33).

From angel Moroni, Joseph learned that,

> God had a work for me to do; and that my name should be had for good and evil among all nations, kindreds, and tongues, or that it should be both good and evil...spoken of among all people.

Joseph was also told of a book written upon plates that had the appearance of gold and of a Urim and Thummim that had been prepared to help him translate the plates. As the angel spoke of these sacred things, "the place [the hill] where the plates were deposited" was shown him in vision. When the illuminating scene ended, the angel departed. Before dawn, however, the angelic messenger reappeared again and again until his visits "occupied the whole of that night" (JS-History 1:33, 42, 47).

The next morning Joseph arose from his bed with plans to go about the "necessary labors of the day" in the fields. He went to the fields on his family farm but in so doing, discovered his strength was gone. As he walked toward the family home, his steps were arrested when the angel again appeared and "related unto me all that he had related to me the previous night, and commanded me to go to my father and tell him of the vision and commandments which I had received."

In compliance, Joseph retraced his steps to the field and told his father Joseph Smith Sr. of the angel and his message. "It was of God," affirmed Father Smith (JS-History 1:48-50). Joseph went to the place shown him in vision—"a hill of considerable size, and the most elevated of any in the neighborhood." On the hill, he discovered that "under a stone of considerable size, lay the plates, deposited in a stone box." He attempted to remove the plates from their receptacle but was prevented by the same heavenly messenger. "The time for bringing them forth had not yet arrived," Joseph was told. The time would not come "until he had learned to keep the commandments of God—not only till he was willing but able to do it" (JS-History 1:51, 53).

Four years passed before 21-year-old Joseph Smith was given the plates and the Urim and Thummim. During that interim, his mother recalled:

> He would describe the ancient inhabitants of this continent, their dress, mode of travelling, and the animals upon which they rode; their cities, their buildings, with every particular; their mode of warfare; and also their religious worship. This he would do with as much ease, seemingly, as if he had spent his whole life among them.[68]

68. Lucy Mack Smith, History, 1845, p. 87.

His brother William was asked, "Did you not doubt Joseph's testimony sometimes?" William replied, "No we all had implicit confidence in what he said. He was a truthful boy. Father and Mother believed him; why should not the children?"[69] The Smith family not only believed Joseph, but were "confirmed in the opinion that God was about to bring to light something upon which we could stay our minds, or that would give us a more perfect knowledge of the plan of salvation and the redemption of the human family." Their conviction of forthcoming truth led Mother Smith to pen, "Tranquility reigned in our midst."[70]

69. "Wm. B. Smith's Last Statement," Zion's Ensign 5 (January 13, 1894), p. 6.

70. Lucy Mack Smith, History, 1845, p. 87.

Unfortunately, tranquility did not last long. A mob element in Palmyra threatened physical violence. The death of Alvin Smith and the marriage of Joseph to

Emma Hale of Harmony, Pennsylvania did not temper the lawless in town. When Joseph received the gold plates on September 27, 1827 "with this charge: that I should be responsible for them; that if I should let them go carelessly, or through any neglect of mine, I should be cut off," it was not an idle warning (JS-History 1:59). "Satan had now stirred up the hearts of those who had gotten a hint of the matter to search into it and make every possible move towards thwarting the purposes of the Almighty." Mobs shouted, "We will have them plates in spite of Joe Smith or all the devils in hell."[71] Knowing of their unbridled determination to get their hands on the plates, Joseph hid the plates in sundry places around the family farm, hoping to keep thieves at bay.

71. Ibid., p 107.

Instead of being frustrated by his tactics, the would-be thieves grew more vigilant in their efforts to obtain the plates. To keep the plates safe, Joseph and his wife, Emma, found it best to leave Palmyra. For a time, they lived at the home of Emma's father, Isaac Hale, in Harmony, Pennsylvania. The Hale home provided a brief respite until Father Hale discovered Joseph had secret contents that he could not see. Joseph and Emma then sought a home of their own in Harmony. In this abode, a son was born who died just a few hours after his birth. Also in this home, the Book of Lehi was translated. The handwritten copy of the translation was stolen due to the carelessness of Martin Harris.

After these tragedies, there came a sense of peace into their home—a blessing associated with translating and scribing the Book of Mormon. Emma recalled, "I am satisfied that no man could have dictated the writing of the manuscripts unless he was inspired."

Explaining the process, Emma continued:

> When acting as his scribe, [he] would dictate to me hour after hour; and when returning after meals, or after interruptions, he would at once begin where he had left off, without either seeing the manuscript or having any portion of it read to him. This was a usual thing for him to do. It would have been improbable that a learned man could do this; and, for one so ignorant and unlearned as he was, it was simply impossible.[72]

72. "Last Testimony of Sister Emma," The Saints' Herald 26 (October 1, 1879), p. 290.

Scribe Oliver Cowdery added:

> These were days never to be forgotten—to sit under the sound of a voice dictated by the inspiration of heaven, awakened the utmost gratitude of this bosom,... to write from his mouth, as he translated, with the Urim and Thummim... the history, or record, called 'The book of Mormon.'[73]

73. "Letters of Oliver Cowdery to William W. Phelps 'Letter 1,'" Messenger and Advocate 1, no. 1 (October 1834); History, 1834-1846, p. 46. Joseph Smith Papers.

On May 15, 1829 Joseph and Oliver "went into the woods to pray and inquire of the Lord respecting baptism for the remission of sins, that we found mentioned in the translation of the plates." While they were praying on the banks of the Susquehanna River, a messenger sent from heaven, known in the New Testament as John the Baptist, "descended in a cloud of light, and having his hands upon us, ordained" the two young men to the Aaronic Priesthood. He commanded that they "go and be baptized," which they did (JS-History 1:68, 70). After his baptism, Joseph "prophesied concerning the rise of this church, and many other things connected with the Church, and this generation of the children of men."[74]

74. History, circa June-October 1839 [Draft 1]. Joseph Smith Papers.

Next came the restoration of the Melchizedek Priesthood by ancient apostles—Peter, James, and John. "I was also present with Joseph," wrote Oliver, "when the higher or Melchizedek Priesthood was conferred by holy angels from on high."[75] With the restoration of the priesthood came the blessing of greater light and knowledge. "Our minds being now enlightened," wrote Joseph, "we began to have the scriptures laid open to our understandings, and the true meaning and intention of their more mysterious passages revealed unto us" (JS-History 1:74).

75. Preston Nibley, Witnesses of the Book of Mormon (Salt Lake City: Stevens and Wallis, 1946), p. 48.

The days of basking in the word of the Lord and receiving priesthood keys from holy messengers ended all too soon for Joseph and Oliver. Persecution, with all its ills, reared in Harmony and forced them to put aside the sacred and solve the pressing issue of safety.

In May 1829 Joseph and Oliver fled from the mob element in Harmony to the farmhouse of Peter Whitmer Sr. in Fayette, New York. Once safely sequestered in the Whitmer home, translation of the Book of Mormon resumed. As completion of the translation neared, three witnesses—Oliver Cowdery, David Whitmer, and Martin Harris—were shown the ancient plates by the angelic messenger.

The witnesses' stirring testimonies of what they had seen and heard moved Joseph to say, "I am not any longer to be entirely alone in the world."[76] Joseph negotiated with Egbert B. Grandin—a Palmyra printer, bookseller, and publisher of the Wayne Sentinel—to print the Book of Mormon manuscript. Initially, Grandin declined, "believing the whole affair to be a wicked imposture and a scheme to defraud Mr. [Martin] Harris."

76. Lucy Mack Smith, History, 1844-1845, Page [11], bk. 8.

The response was the same when Joseph Smith met with Thurlow Weed, former publisher of the Rochester

Daily Telegraph and later editor of the Rochester Anti-Masonic Enquirer. Joseph and Martin Harris called on Elihu F. Marshall, a book publisher in Rochester. Although Marshall agreed to publish the manuscript, his price was out of reach.

Not finding a viable alternative, Joseph asked Martin Harris to secure the publication. Martin considered his request and accepted the financial burden. Joseph and Martin approached publisher E. B. Grandin again, hoping that he would reconsider publishing the Book of Mormon. Grandin took "the advice of several discrete, fair-minded neighbors," who assured him that his connection with the book would be nothing more than a business matter.[77] Their advice and Martin's willingness to enter a contractual agreement led Grandin to change his mind and publish the manuscript.

77. Pomeroy Tucker, Origin, Rise, and Progress of Mormonism: Biography of Its Founders and History of Its Church (NY: D. Appleton and Company, 1867), pp. 51–52.

The Book of Mormon was printed on a Smith Patented Improved Press manufactured by Robert Hoe & Company of New York City. Printing the 296,000 pages of text was slow. One reason for the slow process was that additional type ordered for the job did not arrive from Albany, New York until late November 1829. Other reasons were based on rumors that Martin Harris would not sell his acreage to cover the printing cost or pay the full cost of printing. Grandin was concerned.

Adding to Grandin's concerns, citizens of Palmyra passed a resolution calling on all residents to boycott purchase of the Book of Mormon and asking them to use their influence to prevent others from buying the book. (These were the very months that Brigham, Heber, and others were so depressed in spirit.) Grandin was persuaded to suspend printing the Book of Mormon in January 1830.

On January 16, 1830 Martin Harris and Joseph Smith reached an agreement to sell the Book of Mormon until sufficient copies had been sold to pay the publication costs. Convinced that Martin Harris would make good on his contractual agreement, a relieved E. B. Grandin resumed printing the Book of Mormon. On March 19, 1830, through the Wayne Sentinel, Grandin announced, "The 'Book of Mormon' will be ready for sale in the course of next week." On March 26, 1830 he advertised, "First Public Sale of the Book of Mormon: the above work, containing about 600 pages, large Deuodecimo, is now for sale, wholesale and retail, at the Palmyra Bookstore, by E. B. Grandin."[78] The price of the Book of Mormon was equivalent to the two-day wage of an adult laborer. The price ranged from $1.25 to $1.75 per book.

78. E. B. Grandin, "First Public Sale...," Wayne Sentinel, March 26, 1830.

Joseph Smith was not in Palmyra on March 26, 1830 when Martin Harris gave the first printed copy of the Book of Mormon to his brother Emer Harris. Joseph arrived in town a few days later and was surprised to find Martin crossing the road ahead with "a Bunch of morman Books." Martin greeted him by saying, "'The Books will not sell for no Body wants them.' Joseph says, 'I think they will sell well.'"[79]

79. Martin Harris quote, in Dean C. Jessee, "Joseph Knight's Recollection of Early Mormon History," BYU Studies 17, no. 1 (Autumn 1976), pp. 36-37.

Copies of the Book of Mormon did, in fact, sell well, and before long, there were groups of believers meeting in Palmyra, Fayette, and Colesville, New York. About 50 believers met on Tuesday, April 6, 1830 in the log home of Peter Whitmer Sr. in Fayette for the first meeting of what would become The Church of Jesus Christ of Latter-day Saints. The meeting began with prayer. After the sacrament of the Lord's Supper was blessed and passed to the assembled, "the Holy Ghost was poured out upon us to a very great degree—some prophesied, whilst we all praised the Lord, and rejoiced exceedingly."[80]

80. History, 1838-1856, volume A-1 [23 December 1805-30 August 1834], p. 37.

Twenty-four-year-old Joseph Smith was recognized by the assembled as "a seer, a translator, a prophet, an apostle of Jesus Christ, an elder of the church through the will of God the Father, and the grace of your Lord Jesus Christ" (D&C 21:1).

At the close of the meeting, Father and Mother Smith came forward and requested baptism. At the water's edge, Joseph exclaimed, "Praise to my God! that I lived to see my own father baptized into the true Church of Jesus Christ!"[81] Joseph witnessed other baptisms that day and in the days to follow, for the Church established in Fayette was "like a grain of mustard seed, which a man took, and sowed in his field... when it is grown, it is the greatest among herbs" (Matthew 13:31-32). The newly baptized declared the truthfulness of the Book of Mormon.

81. Lucy Mack Smith, History, 1845, p. 169.

Samuel Smith

Like other members of his family, Samuel Harrison Smith believed in the visions of his brother Joseph. He was baptized on May 25, 1829 by Oliver Cowdery, becoming the third person baptized in this dispensation.

After his baptism, "he returned to his father's house, greatly glorifying and praising God, being filled with the Holy Spirit."[82]

82. History, 1838–1856, volume A-1 [23 December 1805–30 August 1834], p. 19.

At the first Church conference held in June 1830 at Father Peter Whitmer's log home in Fayette, Samuel was ordained an elder. It is a traditional view that he was also set apart at the conference by his brother Joseph to be the first missionary of the Church.

On June 30, 1830 Samuel began a journey to Bloomington, New York with plans to sell copies of the Book of Mormon. His success was almost nil. He was turned away from five different places including an inn where he had hoped to lodge for the night.

Yet Samuel left two copies of the Book of Mormon with members of the extended Young family—one went to Brigham's brother Phinehas and the other was loaned to his sister Rhoda and her husband, the Reverend John P. Greene. Phinehas set aside his labors and "read it twice through, and pronounced it true."[83] Phinehas lent his copy of the Book of Mormon to his father, John Young, who thought it was "the greatest work and the clearest of error of anything he had ever seen, the Bible not excepted."[84]

83. Phinehas Young to Brigham Young, 11 August 1845, Brigham Young Papers.

84. Ibid

Rhoda read the book and declared it "a revelation." Family tradition suggests that Rhoda passed the book to her brother Brigham. "Though I had beheld, all my life, that the traditions of the people was all the religion they had," Brigham said:

> Says I, 'Wait a little while; what is the doctrine of the book, and of the revelations the Lord has given? Let me apply my heart to them;' and after I had done this, I considered it my right to know for myself... I wished time sufficient to prove all things for myself."[85]

85. Brigham Young, "The Gospel of Salvation—A Vision—Redemption of the Earth and all that Pertains to It," Journal of Discourses, 3:91.

He later taught that God did not intend His people "to be led entirely by another person, suspending their own understanding, and pinning their faith upon another's sleeve."

He declared, "It is my duty to know the mind of the Lord concerning myself."[86]
And that was what he did with the Book of Mormon. Although Brigham had the Book of Mormon in his hands about three months after it was published on Grandin's presses in Palmyra, he was slower than his father, John Young, and his siblings, Phinehas and Rhoda, to pronounce the book the word of God.

86. Deseret Weekly News, August 24, 1854, p. 1; Deseret Weekly News, September 22, 1875, p. 4.

87. Brigham Young, "Personal Reminisces, etc.," Journal of Discourses, 8:38.

As Brigham carefully studied the Book of Mormon, he desired to become

> acquainted with the people who professed to believe it... to see whether good common sense was manifest; and if they had that, I wanted them to present it in accordance with the Scriptures.[87]

Thus, in fall of 1831 Brigham and his friend Heber C. Kimball listened attentively to elders of the fledgling Church, who were passing through Mendon from Columbia, Pennsylvania on their way to Kirtland, Ohio. Of them and their Restoration message Brigham said,

> If all the talent, tact, wisdom, and refinement of the world had been sent to me with the Book of Mormon, and had declared, in the most exalted of earthly eloquence, the truth of it, undertaking to prove it by learning, and worldly wisdom, they would have been to me like the smoke which arises only to vanish away. But when I saw a man without eloquence, or talents for public speaking, who could only say, "I know, by the power of the Holy Ghost, that the Book of Mormon is true, that Joseph Smith is a Prophet of the Lord," the Holy Ghost proceeding from that individual illuminated my understanding, and light, glory, and immortality were before me. I was encircled by them, filled with them, and I knew for myself that the testimony of the man was true... My own judgment, natural endowments, and education bowed to this simple, but mighty testimony.[88]

88. Brigham Young, "March of "Mormonism"—The Power of God and the Wisdom of Man—Good and Evil Influences—The Law of Increase," Journal of Discourses, 1:90.

According to Heber C. Kimball, he and Brigham were "constrained by the Spirit to bear testimony of the truth which we had heard, and when we did this, the power of God rested upon us and we had a testimony that the work was true."[89]

89. See "History of Brigham Young," MS no. 1, in Esplin, "Conversion and Transformation: Brigham Young's New York Routes and the Search for Bible Religion," p. 180.

After the elders bid farewell, Heber accompanied Brigham and his brother Joseph, and their father, John Young, to the woods to cut wood for Phinehas Young. As they labored, Heber reflected again and again on what the elders had told them, especially the part about the gathering of the Saints. He then saw in vision "the gathering of the Saints to Zion, and the glory that would rest upon them; and many more things connected with that great event, such as the sufferings and persecutions which would come upon the people of God, and the calamities and judgments which would come upon the world."[90] Heber interpreted the vision as a witness that the message of the Restoration was of God.

90. "Synopsis of the History of Heber Chase Kimball," p. 25. Church History Library.

Yet Heber C. Kimball and Brigham Young delayed being baptized. They had read the Book of Mormon, listened to elders from the Church of Christ, and had visions in the day and night, but they had never attended a Church meeting or seen a worship service. Heber proposed to Brigham and his brother Phinehas that they use his horse and sleigh and journey to where the elders had been preaching in Pennsylvania and visit members in their homes.

Brigham was enthusiastic about the idea. He wanted to meet those "who professed to believe [the Book of Mormon]" and to judge whether their lives reflected the fruits of the doctrine of the Restoration or were as those he had known in his youth—sober and soft spoken on the Sabbath Day but not Christians in their walk.[91]

91. Brigham Young, "Personal Reminisces, etc.," Journal of Discourses, 8:38.

Brigham, Heber, and Phinehas journeyed to Columbia, located in the northwestern section of Pennsylvania. As to what they discovered among members,

Brigham said:

> We stayed with the church the[re] about six days, attended their meetings, heard them speak in tongues, interpret and prophecy: these things truly caused us to rejoice and praise the Lord. We returned home being convinced of the truth of these things . . . and bore testimony to the truth of those things which we had seen and heard to our friends and neighbors.[92]

92. "History of Brigham Young," in Esplin, "Conversion and Transformation: Brigham Young's New York Routes and the Search for Bible Religion," p. 181.

Once Brigham was satisfied with the truth of the prophetic calling of Joseph Smith and the coming forth of the Book of Mormon, he desired to share his newfound beliefs with his older brother Joseph Young. Brigham characterized his brother as a solemn man of sad heart, a "very spiritual man" who was always praying.

Like Brigham, after seeking wisdom and solace from the Bible, Joseph had concluded that there were no "Bible Christians" on the earth. The conclusion left him in despair; he neither laughed nor smiled. "I do not see any possible escape for the human family," Joseph announced, "all must go to perdition."

In February 1832, Brigham, accompanied by his brother-in-law John P. Greene part of the way, journeyed by horse and sleigh 200 miles to see his brother Joseph Young, who was preaching Methodism in Upper Canada. As they journeyed, Brigham and John P. Greene discussed the truths of the Restoration. Brigham told John, "If you don't get snagged I'll treat."[93]

93. Minutes, 8 January 1845, General Minutes Collection, in Esplin, "Conversion and Transformation: Brigham Young's New York Routes and the Search for Bible Religion," p. 182.

Once in Canada, Brigham explained to his brother Joseph Young his feelings about the "folly and nonsense so prevalent in the Christian world" and about the truths found in the Book of Mormon, among converts, and the Restoration message of the missionaries.

Joseph Young remembered that Brigham also reported:

> Many things of interest concerning the signs and wonderful mericals [sic] being wrought through the believers in this new faith. I was ripe for receiving something that would feed my mental cravings, and this seemed to be the food I wanted—nothing could have been more acceptable to my poor famishing soul. I hailed it as my spiritual jubilee—a deliverance from a long night of darkness and bondage.[94]

94. "Journal of Joseph Young, Sr.," in Joseph Young Sr. Collection. Church History Library.

Joseph Young arranged his affairs and left his Canadian Methodist ministry to return with Brigham to Mendon, New York. In the month of March 1832, shortly after their arrival, Joseph accompanied his father John Young and his brother Phinehas to Pennsylvania, where all three were baptized members of the Church of Christ.

Brigham was notably absent on that occasion. Why? He later told his family, "I could get to the bottom of all the religions that I have any knowledge of, but this I reasoned on month after month . . . This was out of my reach."[95] Brigham further explained:

95. Minutes, 8 January 1845. Brigham Young Papers; Brigham Young, "Saints Subject to Temptation—True Riches, Virtue, and Sanctification—"Mormonism"—Gladdenites, Apostles, and Saints—Devils without Tabernacles," Journal of Discourses, 2:123-124.

> I examined the matter studiously, for two years, before I made up my mind to receive that book. I knew it was true, as well as I knew that I could see with my eyes, or feel by the touch of my fingers, or be sensible of the demonstration of any sense. Had not this been the case, I never would have embraced it. . . . It would have all been without form or comeliness to me. I wished time sufficient to prove all things for myself.[96]

96. Brigham Young, "Cultivate Forbearance," Millennial Star, July 11, 1892, 441-442.

Reading the Book of Mormon and listening to missionaries brought answers, but Brigham wanted more.

He delved into the matter of baptism as perhaps few converts in the 1830s had done. He said, "I could not more honestly and earnestly have prepared myself to go into eternity than I did to come into this Church; and when I had ripened everything in my mind, I drank it in, and not till then. From that day to this, it is all right with me."[97]

97. Brigham Young, "Personal Reminisces, etc.," Journal of Discourses, 8:38.

"Were you to ask me how it was that I embraced 'Mormonism,'" Brigham said, "I should answer, for the simple reason that it embraces all truth in heaven and on earth." Mormonism to him was "light, intelligence, power, and truth."[98]

98. Arrington, Brigham Young, American Moses, pp. 28-29.

Baptism

On the snowy day of April 14, 1832, Eleazer Miller, one of the elders who had preached in Pennsylvania, baptized Brigham, who had walked two miles in a storm to the small millstream to be baptized. (The stream was probably the very stream that Brigham had put in a waterwheel to power his mill machinery on his father's property in Mendon.) On the water's edge, Elder Miller conferred upon Brigham the Holy Ghost and ordained him an elder. Speaking of his ordination to the Melchizedek Priesthood, Brigham said, "According to the words of the Savior, I felt a humble, child-like spirit, witnessing to me that my sins were forgiven."[99]

99. Young, Here is Brigham . . . , p. 60.

From that point on, Brigham "never look[ed] back upon the old world [for] it is like looking into Hell."[100]

100. Minutes, 7 April 1850. General Minutes Collection.

He said, "I did not embrace Mormonism because I hoped it was true, but because I knew it was that principle that would save all the human family that would obey it."[101] "Had I not so learned this truth, I

101. "Minutes of General Conference," Millennial Star 12, no. 18 (September 15, 1850), p. 275.

should never have been what is called a 'Mormon.'"[102] The gloom and despair that had surrounded Brigham since childhood was lifted. He was now filled with "good feelings, with joy rejoicing."[103]

His biographer Ronald K. Esplin wrote, "Hope and purpose replaced discouragement as if a curtain had been removed from the face of the sun. Instead of sorrow and grief, suddenly it became 'Glory! Hallelujah! Praise God!'"[104]

Three weeks after his baptism, Brigham's wife Miriam entered baptismal waters as did many of Brigham's relatives and friends.

Preacher of the Gospel of Jesus Christ

After his baptism, Brigham wanted to speak of his witness of the Book of Mormon and the Restoration message. His initiation as a speaker came the week after he entered baptismal waters. At a meeting with several seasoned elders present, he recalled:

> I was about as destitute of language as a man could well be... I was but a child, so far as public speaking and a knowledge of the world was concerned; but the Spirit of the Lord was upon me, and I felt as though my bones would consume within me unless I spoke to the people and told them what I had seen, heard and learned—what I had experienced and rejoiced in; and the first discourse I ever delivered I occupied over an hour. I opened my mouth and the Lord filled it... [105]

From that initial experience, Brigham concluded the Lord would fill his mouth with the Restoration message

102. Brigham Young, "Apostleship of Joseph Smith—Destruction Awaiting the Nations," Journal of Discourses, 9:364-365.

103. Brigham Young, "Disinclination of Men to Learn Through the Teachings and Experience of Others—Latter-Day Saints Compared With Those of Former Days—Sacrifice—Sheep and Goats—Customs and Traditions," Journal of Discourses, 3:320.

104. Esplin, "Conversion and Transformation: Brigham Young's New York Routes and the Search for Bible Religion," p. 185.

105. Brigham Young, "Joseph Smith's Family—Bashfulness in Public Speaking—The Coming Crisis—Counsel," Journal of Discourses, 5:97; Brigham Young, "Preaching the Gospel—The Principles and Spirit of the Same," Journal of Discourses, 13:211.

of truth and light:

> When I have endeavored to address a congregation, I have almost always felt a repugnance in my heart to the practice of premeditation, or of preconstructing a discourse to deliver to the people, but let me ask God my heavenly Father, in the name of Jesus Christ, to give me His Spirit, and put into my heart the things He wishes me to speak whether they be for better or worse. . . . I would ask . . . that we might speak and hear with an understanding heart, that a hint, a key word, or a short sentence pertaining to the things of God, might open the vision of our minds, so that we might comprehend the things of eternity, and rejoice exceedingly therein.[106]

106. Brigham Young, "True and False Riches," Journal of Discourses, 1:264.

Brigham summarized his missionary labors in the spring and summer of 1832 by saying, "Seven months had scarce passed away when there was a dozen branches raised up."[107] After summer had passed, he traveled twice to Canada preaching along the way. "I wanted to thunder and roar out the Gospel to the nations," he said:

107. Brigham Young, "History," manuscripts no. 1, 3, Minutes of Family Meeting, 8 January 1845, in Arrington, Brigham Young, American Moses, p. 35.

> It burned in my bones like fire pent up... Nothing would satisfy me but to cry abroad in the world, what the Lord was doing in the latter-days... I had to go out and preach, lest my bones should consume within me.[108]

108. Brigham Young, "The Privileges and Blessings of the Gospel," Journal of Discourses, 1:313.

His preaching from town to town ended abruptly when Brigham learned that his wife Miriam had contracted tuberculosis. He assumed much of the burden of running a household and caring for the children. As Miriam progressively became more impaired, Brigham regularly prepared breakfast for his family, cleaned the house, and "carried his wife to the rocking chair by the fireplace and left her there until he could return in the evening."[109] He cooked dinner, put the children to bed, and finished necessary household chores. His experience in caring for his children, tending to a sick wife, and managing a home led him to boast that he could beat "most of the women in [the] community at housekeeping."[110]

In September 1832, less than five months after her baptism, Miriam Works Young died of tuberculosis, leaving Brigham alone to care for their two daughters. Needing help, Brigham and his daughters moved into the Heber C. Kimball home. For 18 months Heber's wife Vilate mothered her namesake—Vilate Young and her older sister Elizabeth Young.

After disestablishing his household after Miriam's death and having Vilate care for his daughters, Brigham gave away many of his possessions and significantly decreased his woodworking business. His reason for so doing—he wanted to be unencumbered so he could preach the message of the Restoration. He also wanted to be free to travel to Kirtland, Ohio to meet the Prophet Joseph Smith.

109. Susa Young Gates, The Life Story of Brigham Young: Mormon Leader, Founder of Salt Lake City, and Builder of an Empire in the Uncharted Wastes of Western America (1930), p. 5.

110. Deseret News Weekly, August 12, 1857, p. 4.

Brigham Young, about 1846; copy of a daguerreotype by Lucain R. Foster.

Chapter Three
Gathering to Kirtland

Brigham was not the only new convert going from village to village declaring the truth of the Book of Mormon. Dozens of men who had recently entered baptismal waters were proclaiming the Restoration message, taking self-appointed missionary journeys, and strengthening fledgling branches of the Church. Young and old, learned and illiterate listened and embraced the revelatory teachings espoused by the converts.

Among their number were seekers like Warren Foote, who wrote, "[I] frequently prayed to the Lord in secret to guide me in the right way."[111] After listening to the Restoration message and comparing the words of the Book of Mormon with biblical verse, Foote entered baptismal waters and began his own missionary efforts.

111. Andrew Jenson, Latter-day Saints Biographical Encyclopedia 4 vols. (Salt Lake City: Deseret News, 1901-1936), 1:376.

Thus, the message of the Restoration spread from person to person and from village to village in New York, Pennsylvania, and Ohio.

Parley P. Pratt, one of the first missionaries to bring news of the Restoration to Ohio, reported, "The people thronged us night and day, insomuch that we had no time for rest or retirement."[112] Most notable among the throng was Sidney Rigdon. Having been a Baptist preacher and a founder of the Campbellite movement, Rigdon was curious yet skeptical about the Restoration message until he read the Book of Mormon.

112. Parley P. Pratt, ed., Autobiography of Parley Parker Pratt (Salt Lake City: Deseret Book, 1980), p. 48.

Convinced of the eternal truths contained in the Book of Mormon, Rigdon was baptized.

Others followed until they numbered an estimated 127 converts in the Kirtland area. A few Ohio converts clung to outward practices of their former religions, contending that physical demonstrations were a reflection of the gifts of the Spirit. At Church worship services, they would

> swoon away, and make unseemly gestures, and be drawn or disfigured in their countenances. Others would fall into ecstasies, and be drawn into contortions, cramps, fits, etc. Others would seem to have visions and revelations, which were not edifying, and which were not congenial to the doctrine and spirit of the Gospel.[113]

113. Ibid., p. 61.

Take for instance, a man known only as Black Pete. He claimed to see angels and to receive letters directly from heaven. George A. Smith wrote of Black Pete running "off a steep wash bank twenty-five feet high" and falling into the Chagrin River trying to catch a flying revelation.[114] Heman Basset claimed to receive a revelation from an angel. After reading the revelation to others, he showed a picture of what he said was a group of angels. Then there was Mrs. Hubble who professed to be a "prophetess of the Lord."[115]

114. George A. Smith, "Historical Discourse," Journal of Discourses, 11:3-4.

115. John Whitmer, History, 1831–circa 1847, p. 11. Joseph Smith Papers.

Failure to discern between the strange notions and false spirits led to differences of opinion and doctrinal confusion among converts in Kirtland, Ohio. So confused were the newly baptized that some converts expressed aloud their belief that only the Prophet Joseph, himself, could set the Church in order. Among the converts were Newel and Elizabeth Whitney. About midnight one evening as the Whitneys were praying to know how to receive the Holy Ghost and discern right from wrong in worship services, Elizabeth said,

> The Spirit rested upon us and a cloud overshadowed the house. It was as though we were out of doors. The house passed away from our vision... A solemn awe pervaded us. We saw the cloud and felt the Spirit of the Lord. Then we heard a voice out of the cloud saying, "Prepare to receive the word of the Lord for it is coming."[116]

116. Jenson, LDS Biographical Encyclopedia, 1:223.

The Doctrine of Gathering

In December 1830, eight months after the organization of the Church, Joseph Smith received a revelation calling Church members in New York to "assemble together at the Ohio" (D&C 37:32). To assemble meant to gather. Some of the New York Saints accepted the call as the word of God while others refused to acknowledge the directive as coming from the Lord.

At the third conference of the Church held at Fayette, New York, the Prophet Joseph received a revelation "in the presence of the whole congregation" confirming the doctrine of gathering to Ohio was from the Lord: "Go to the Ohio; and there I will give unto you my law; and there you shall be endowed with power from on high" (D&C 38:32).

Joseph Smith and his wife Emma were the first of the New York Saints to arrive in Kirtland. On or about February 1, 1831, they pulled up in front of the N. K. Whitney and Company store. As Joseph alighted from the sleigh, he said to the man sweeping snow from the porch, "Newel K. Whitney! Thou art the man!" Joseph then extended his hand as if they were old acquaintances. "You have the advantage of me," Newel replied, "I could not call you by name, as you have me." Joseph said, "I am Joseph Smith, the Prophet. You've prayed me

117. Ibid.

here; now what do you want of me?"[117]

Within a few months of Joseph Smith's arrival in Kirtland, other Saints from New York began their journey. Saints residing in Colesville, New York rendezvoused at Ithaca, New York and began their journey via the port at Cayuga Lake, embarking on April 25, 1831.

Close behind the Colesville Saints was Lucy Mack Smith with the Fayette Branch of the Church. Her contingent left Seneca County, New York by boat at the Kingdom (a small unincorporated community between Waterloo and Seneca Falls) on the Cayuga-Seneca Canal traveling on to Buffalo.

A third canal boat with 30 more of their fellow Saints from the Palmyra/Manchester area led by Thomas B. Marsh were soon on their way. During the week of May 15-21, about 50 Saints under the direction of Martin Harris left Palmyra. The editor of the Wayne Sentinel, Egbert B. Grandin, wrote of their exodus on May 27, 1831:

> Several families, numbering about fifty souls, took up their line of march from this town last week for the "promised land," among whom was Martin Harris, one of the original believers in the "Book of Mormon." Mr. Harris was among the early settlers of this town, and has ever borne the character of an honorable and upright man, and an obliging and benevolent neighbor. He had secured to himself by honest industry a respectable fortune—and he has left a large circle of acquaintances to pity his delusion.[118]

118. "Mormonism and Martin Harris," Wayne Sentinel, May 27, 1831, p. 3.

By June 1831 so many followers of Joseph Smith had arrived in Ohio, the editor of the Painesville Telegraph expressed discomfort at seeing "about two hundred men, women and children, of the deluded followers of Jo Smith's Bible speculation, have arrived on our coast... from New York." With his wife entering baptismal waters, the editor feared, "If the growth of the Church were not soon halted, inhabitants of Kirtland would be governed by the revelations of the Mormon Prophet."[119] As the numbers swelled, one contemporary wrote:

119. "Mormon Emigration," Painesville Telegraph, May 17, 1831.

> They came, men, women, and children, in every conceivable manner, some with horses, oxen, and vehicles rough and rude, while others had walked all or part of the distance. The future "City of the Saints" appeared like one besieged. Every available house, shop, hut, or barn was filled to its utmost capacity. Even boxes were roughly extemporized and used for shelter until something more permanent could be secured.[120]

120. "Mormonism and Martin Harris," Wayne Sentinel, May 27, 1831, p. 3.

Whatever their economic circumstance, neither poverty nor discomfort stopped the flow of the faithful to Ohio. Among those who gathered was John P. Greene and his wife Rhoda. They were the first of Brigham's extended family to sell property in Mendon, New York so they could gather with the Saints. Other family members were talking of Ohio and making similar plans. Brigham was not ready to make such plans, but he did want to meet the Prophet Joseph Smith.

Brigham Young meets Joseph Smith

About three weeks after Miriam's funeral, Brigham and his brother Joseph Young and friend Heber C. Kimball took a team of horses and a wagon and journeyed 325 miles from Mendon to Kirtland to meet Joseph Smith. Along their travel route, they strengthened fledgling

Church branches. "We exhorted them and prayed with them, and I spoke in tongues," Brigham wrote. "Some pronounced it genuine and from the Lord, and others pronounced it of the Devil."[121]

121. Brigham Young, "History of Brigham Young," Millennial Star 25 (July 11, 1863), p. 439.

The traveling party arrived in Kirtland in early November 1832 and lodged with John and Rhoda Greene. After resting briefly at the Greene's home, the threesome went to find Joseph Smith. "We went to [Joseph Smith's] father's house," Brigham wrote. There they learned that "[the Prophet Joseph] was in the woods" just behind the Newel K. Whitney home. They hastened into the woods near the east branch of the Chagrin River to find him.[122] Brigham wrote:

122. Watson, Manuscript History of Brigham Young, p. 4.

> We found the Prophet, and two or three of his brothers, chopping and hauling wood. Here my joy was full at the privilege of shaking the hand of the Prophet of God, and received the sure testimony, by the Spirit of prophecy, that he was all that any man could believe him to be, as a true Prophet. He was happy to see us, and bid us welcome.[123]

123. Ibid., p. 4.

The Prophet Joseph then "threw down his ax, and... we went with him to his house. He introduced us to his wife Emma; who was in bed with the infant, Joseph."[124]

124. Joseph Young to Lewis Harvey, November 16, 1880. L. Tom Perry Special Collections, Harold B. Lee Library, Brigham Young University, Provo, UT.

Brigham, Heber, and Joseph Young stayed in to the evening hours at Joseph's home. They were there when some of the brethren came wanting to discuss "the things of the kingdom."[125]

125. "History of Brigham Young," Deseret News, February 10, 1858, p. 385, reprinted in Brigham Young, "History of Brigham Young," Millennial Star 15 (1864), p. 439.

Brigham recalled that a meeting ensued and "the Prophet called upon me to pray; in my prayer I spoke in tongues."[126] This was the first time Joseph "had heard this Gift among the brethren." Singing in tongues had been heard previously, but not speaking in

126. Watson, Manuscript History of Brigham Young, pp. 4-5.

tongues.[127] Brigham said:

> As soon as we arose from our knees the brethren flocked around [Joseph] and asked his opinion concerning the gift of tongues that was upon me. He told them it was the pure Adamic language. Some said to him they expected he would condemn the gift Brother Brigham had, but he said, "No, it is of God, and the time will come when brother Brigham Young will preside over this Church." The latter part of this conversation was in my absence.[128]

Historian Leonard J. Arrington added:

> During the course of the evening the Prophet, who had never before heard speaking in tongues, received the gift himself. Those present remembered this event as a modern replication of "the day of Pentecost," when the early apostles were "filled with the Holy Spirit, and began to speak with other tongues, as the Spirit gave them utterance."[129]

Brigham's Reaction to meeting Joseph Smith

As to meeting the Prophet Joseph Smith, Brigham wrote:

> I never saw any one, until I met Joseph Smith, who could tell me anything about the character, personality and dwelling place of God, or anything satisfactory about angels, or the relationship of man to his Maker. Yet I was as diligent as any man need to be to try and find out those things.[130]

> [Joseph Smith] took heaven, figuratively speak-

127. Minutes, Discourse, and Blessings, 1 March 1835, p. 179, footnote 35. Joseph Smith Papers.

128. Brigham Young, in "History of Brigham Young," Millennial Star, July 11, 1863, p. 439.

129. Arrington, Brigham Young, American Moses, p. 34.

130. Brigham Young, "Unbelief—The Saints Require Constant Instruction—Contrast Between the Gospel of Christ and the Religions of Men—Evil would Cease among the Saints if They would Live their Religion—Gathering the Poor—Tithing—Knowledge of God—Progress of the Work is Due to the Operations of the Spirit," Journal of Discourses, 16:46.

ing, and brought it down to earth; and he took the earth, brought it up, and opened up, in plainness and simplicity, the things of God; and that is the beauty of his mission.[131]

131. Brigham Young, "Testimony of the Spirit—Revelation Given According to Requirements—Spiritual Warfare and Conquest, etc.," Journal of Discourses, 5: 322.

Brigham summarized his belief in Joseph Smith's prophetic calling by saying, "When I first heard him preach, he brought heaven and earth together."[132] He further said:

132. John A. Widtsoe, Discourses of Brigham Young (Salt Lake City: Deseret Book, 1941), p. 458.

> I can truly say, that I invariably found him to be all that any people could require a true prophet to be, and that a better man could not be, though he had his weaknesses; and what man has ever lived upon this earth who had none?"[133]

133. Brigham Young to David B. Smith, June 1, 1853, in Arrington, Brigham Young, American Moses, p. 60.

Brigham further said of Joseph Smith:

> I feel like shouting Hallelujah, all the time, when I think that I ever knew Joseph Smith, the Prophet whom the Lord raised up and ordained, and to whom he gave keys and power to build up the Kingdom of God on the earth and sustain it."[134]

134. Widstoe, Discourses of Brigham Young, p. 458.

As time passed Brigham held the opinion

> The Lord had his eyes upon [Joseph Smith], and upon his father, and upon his father's father, and upon their progenitors clear back to Abraham, and from Abraham to the flood, from the flood to Enoch, and from Enoch to Adam. He has watched that family and that blood as it has circulated from its fountain to the birth of that man. He was fore-ordained in eternity to preside over this last dispensation.[135]

135. Ibid., p. 108.

> [The Lord] called upon his servant Joseph Smith, Jr., when he was but a boy, to lay the foundation of his Kingdom for the last time. Why did he call upon Joseph Smith to do it? Because he was disposed to do it. Was Joseph Smith the only person on earth who could have done this work? No doubt there were many others who, under the direction of the Lord, could have done that work; but the Lord selected the one that pleased him, and that is sufficient.[136]

136. Ibid., p. 460.

Not in Joseph's Inner Circle

Even though Brigham had spoken in tongues and Joseph Smith had interpreted his words to mean that he would live to preside over the Church, Brigham was not swept up into what some historians have called "Joseph's inner circle."

Longtime associates and newfound friends like Oliver Cowdery, Sidney Rigdon, Frederick G. Williams, Newel K. Whitney and Joseph's brother Hyrum Smith were in the inner circle, not Brigham. Brigham was not even encouraged to return to Mendon and bring his children to Kirtland so they could gather as a family to Ohio. He was not invited to remain in Kirtland for the winter months to attend the School of the Prophets. Instead, Brigham was encouraged to leave Kirtland and spread the word for others "to gather."

This may seem peculiar as Joseph had prophesied that Brigham would one day preside over the Church. It is easy to suppose that Joseph would want Brigham by his side learning how to guide the affairs of the Church. Such was not the case in November 1832. Joseph would remain in Kirtland where he would lead the Church, and Brigham was to resume his missionary work.

Brigham, his brother Joseph Young, and Heber C. Kimball remained in Kirtland for only a week. During that week, Brigham recalled:

> [We] held meetings nearly every night, and the blessings of the Lord were extensively upon us. I baptized one man while in Kirtland, by the name of Gibson Smith, the father of Newel K. Whitney's wife, who had just come from Connecticut to learn the things that were being revealed. Being convinced of the truth of the work, he requested me to go into the waters with him.[137]

137. Watson, Manuscript History of Brigham Young, p. 4.

Before the threesome departed from Kirtland, the Prophet Joseph Smith was told of Artemus Millett, a skilled stonemason whom Joseph Young had known in Upper Canada. The Prophet asked Joseph Young to go to Upper Canada and baptize Artemus Millett and ask him to gather to Kirtland. Joseph Young accepted the call, a mission that Brigham felt compelled to serve as well. The three men then headed back to Mendon, preaching in small Church branches along their route and feeling well-paid for their efforts to meet the Prophet Joseph.

Mission to Upper Canada

Less than a month after returning to Mendon, Brigham had joined his brother Joseph Young in heading to Upper Canada. The brothers traveled over 500 miles on foot in December 1832, most of the way through snow from one to two feet deep. They crossed six miles of thin ice on the east end of Lake Ontario (where the St. Lawrence River begins) to reach Kingston, Canada. There, Brigham wrote briefly of his missionary experience:

> We commenced preaching and bearing our testimony to the people. Proceeding [north] to West Loboro, we remained about one month preaching the Gospel there and in the regions round about. We baptized about 45 souls, and organized the West Loboro and other Branches. In the month of February 1833, we started for home, crossing from Kingston on the ice, just before it broke up.[138]

138. Ibid., p. 5.

Although it was Joseph Young who had received the mission call from the Prophet to baptize Artemus Millett, it was his companion Brigham, who baptized him on February 18, 1833 in Loboro, Canada. The summer of 1833, Brother Millett sold his property and moved to Kirtland to help build a temple to God.

As for Brigham, he returned to Mendon and again lived with the Heber C. Kimball family. By early spring, he was ready for a change but not ready to gather to Ohio. He took his children to the home of their maternal grandmother in Aurelius, New York. When his daughters were comfortable in the care of their aging grandmother, Brigham preached in Aurelius and Auburn to old acquaintances.

After a month, Brigham extended his preaching into Upper Canada where he met with old friends, baptizing many, and visiting Church branches. He also organized a new branch. He wrote brief diary entries of his activities in Canada:

> 29) Monday went to Lob[o]ro. Had a prair meting in the evening, found the Brotherin in good helth and in good Sperits. Their has been 17 Seventeen Baptized sence Brother Joseph and I left their...

30) thursday went to Brother N. Lake. Held a meting at one o'clock. Had good liberty in preaching.

June 1,th 1833 preached at 10 A.M. at Peater Rice's—took Dinner at Brother Picksley's, then attended Reform Methodist quarteley meting in the afternoon.

2) Sunday held meting at Brother Daniel Wood at 10 A.M. At 4 P.M. at Stiles' barn and Baptized three….

8) Saterday met in confrence with seven Elders… two teachers ordained….

17) Preached at the Loge schoole house west of Brother Mil[l]et's.[139]

139. Manuscript Diary, 1832-1835, Brigham Young Papers, in England, Brother Brigham, pp. 20-21.

Before returning to Aurelius and to his children, Brigham escorted several Canadian converts to Kirtland. While there, he visited the Prophet Joseph Smith again. It was clear that Joseph had grown in confidence of Brigham and his missionary efforts, for he immediately called him to take his brother Joseph Young on a journey to New England to preach to extended family members and friends.

Although in debt and without a home or a place to set up his woodworking shop, and having been absent from his daughters for over a month, Brigham did not hesitate to fulfill the calling. "It has never entered into my heart," he declared when later remembering the Prophet's requests, "from the first day I was called to preach the Gospel to this day, when the Lord said, 'Go and leave your family,' to offer the least objection."[140]

140. Brigham Young, "The Word of Wisdom especially suited to Infants and Youth—Privations in Missouri—Necessity of Integrity, and Strife for Excellence—Responsibility of Parents," Journal of Discourses, 2:19.

Brigham gathers to Kirtland

After preaching in the eastern states with his brother Joseph Young from July through September 1833, Brigham boarded a small boat on the Erie Canal heading to Aurelius to retrieve his children. With daughters in his arms, in September 1833 Brigham now expressed an insatiable desire to gather with Saints of God in Kirtland. He believed his work in spreading the Restoration message and the doctrine of gathering was finished for the time being.

He wanted to be near the Prophet Joseph Smith in Kirtland. He wanted his children to be close. Brigham and his daughters returned to Mendon to gather their belongings and ship them via the Erie Canal to the Fairport Harbor on Lake Erie. By the end of September 1833, Brigham and Heber C. Kimball and their families were on their way to what some were calling, "The City of the Saints." Brigham wrote:

> When we did arrive in Kirtland, if any man that ever did gather with the Saints was any poorer than I was—it was because he had nothing. . . . I had two children to take care of—that was all. I was a widower. "Brother Brigham, had you any shoes?" No; not a shoe to my foot, except a pair of borrowed boots. I had no winter clothing, except a homemade coat that I had had three or four years. "Any pantaloons?" No. "What did you do? Did you go without?" No; I borrowed a pair to wear till I could get another pair. I had travelled and preached and given away every dollar of my property. I was worth a little property when I started to preach. . . . I had traveled and preached until I had nothing left to gather with; but Joseph said: "come up"; and I went up the best I could.[141]

141. Brigham Young, Deseret News: Semi-Weekly, March 9, 1867.

Fall and winter of 1833, Brigham remained in Kirtland. He reported, "I tarried all winter, and had the privilege of listening to the teachings of the Prophet and enjoying the society of the Saints, working hard at my former trade."[142]

142. Watson, Manuscript History of Brigham Young, p. 7.

Although he was impoverished, these were some of Brigham's happiest days. When a few Saints suggested there was more money to be had for his trade outside of Kirtland, he refused to leave. He remained in Kirtland and later said:

> I told them I had gathered to Kirtland because I was so directed by the Prophet of God, and I was not going away . . . anywhere else to build up the Gentiles, but I was going to stay here and seek the things that pertained to the kingdom of God by listening to the teachings of his servants, and I should work for my brethren and trust in God and them that I would be paid. I labored for brother [Reynolds] Cahoon and finished his house, and although he did not know he could pay me when I commenced, before I finished he had me paid in full. I then went to work for father John Smith and others, who paid me, and sustained myself in Kirtland, and when the brethren who had gone out to work for the Gentiles returned, I had means, though some of them were scant.[143]

143. Ibid.

The Kirtland Temple

In January 1831 the Lord commanded Joseph Smith to gather the Saints to Ohio, for there they would be endowed "with power from on high" (D&C 38:32). To receive the endowed power, a temple—"a house of prayer, a house of fasting, a house of faith, a house of learning, a house of glory, a house of order, a house of God" was needed (D&C 88:119). One Latter-day Saint suggested to Joseph Smith that the House of God—the temple—be built of logs. "Shall we, brethren, build a house for our God, of logs?" Joseph asked. "No," he retorted, "I have a better plan than that. I have a plan of the house of the Lord, given by himself."[144]

The Lord's plan for the Kirtland Temple was intricate and multi-faceted in design. Although the external design was similar to other houses of worship at the time, plans for the interior design were unique. The interior was to be 55 feet wide and 65 five feet long with a lower and a higher court.

The lower court (the first floor) was to be dedicated "for your sacrament offering, and for your preaching, and your fasting, and your praying, and the offering up of your most holy desires unto me, saith your Lord." The higher court (the second floor) was to be dedicated for "the school of mine apostles" (D&C 95:16–17). Within each court, two separate four-tiered pulpits were to accommodate presidencies of the Melchizedek and Aaronic Priesthoods.

"Notwithstanding the Church was poor and there was not a scraper and hardly a plow that could be found among the Saints," the followers of Joseph Smith moved forward to build the temple Joseph had envisioned.[145] On June 5, 1833 "George A. Smith hauled the first load of stone" from the quarry, and Hyrum Smith struck "the first blow upon the house."[146]

Helping 15-year-old George A. Smith was Brigham Young and his brother Lorenzo D. Young and Reynolds Cahoon.[147] Since God had commanded Joseph to build a temple, Brigham wanted to help in any way possible. From that point on, Lucy Mack Smith wrote, "There

144. Lucy Mack Smith, History, 1845, p. 226. Joseph Smith Papers.

145. Benjamin F. Johnson, My Life's Review: Autobiography of Benjamin Franklin Johnson (Independence, MO: Zion's Printing and Publishing, 1947), pp. 10-11.

146. History, 1838-1856, volume A-1 [23 December 1805-30 August 1834], p. 302.

147. Roger D. Launius, The Kirtland Temple a Historical Narrative (Independence, MO.: Herald Publishing House, 1986), p. 41.

148. Lucy Mack Smith, History, 1845, p. 227.

was but one mainspring to all our thoughts and actions; and that was, the building of the Lord's house."[148]

Brigham had the needed skills to create windows, paint the interior, and complete delicate woodwork. Few worked with such diligence on the temple as he. Yet, in winter 1834, when he learned that the School of the Prophets was beginning again and he had the opportunity to learn of heavenly matters, his daily routine of working on the temple changed.

In the morning hours, he attended the School of the Prophets that met above the N. K. Whitney and Company store. The meetings were presided over by the Prophet, and each began with a formal greeting, with new attendees welcomed by the ordinance of washing of feet. Then the educational component began. Brigham received a secular education in history, current events, reading and writing, and mathematics. He received a spiritual education, learning doctrinal teachings and receiving manifestations of the Holy Ghost.
Of the school, Brigham wrote:

> The brethren came to [the N. K. Whitney and Company store] for hundreds of miles to attend school in a little room probably no larger than eleven by fourteen. When they assembled together in this room after breakfast, the first they did was to light their pipes, and, while smoking, talk about the great things of the kingdom, and spit all over the room, and as soon as the pipe was out of their mouths a large chew of tobacco would then be taken. Often when the Prophet entered the room to give the school instructions he would then find himself in a cloud of tobacco smoke.[149]

149. Brigham Young, "School of The Prophets—Improvement of Provo City—Litigation—Injudicious Trading," Journal of Discourses, 12:158.

Emma Smith was not pleased. According to David

Whitmer, she remarked to Joseph, "It would be a good thing if a revelation could be had declaring the use of tobacco a sin, and commanding its suppression." Whitmer recalled, The matter was taken up and joked about, one of the brethren suggested that the revelation should also provide for a total abstinence from tea and coffee drinking, intending this as a counter dig at the sisters.[150]

For the Prophet Joseph, the issue was a matter of prayer. On February 27, 1833 he received the Word of Wisdom from the Lord and learned that "tobacco is not for the body, neither for the belly" (D&C 89:8).

Although some of the brethren took this revelation, and others, lightly, Brigham never doubted Joseph's revelatory powers in this or any other revelation. Sitting at the Prophet's feet in this atmosphere of inspired teaching, Brigham entered into a period of relative peace and, indeed, higher education that would serve him well in the responsibilities he would soon be called to bear.

Between attending the School of the Prophets, building the Kirtland Temple, and accepting woodworking jobs in Kirtland, Brigham was busy. Familial sociality with his brothers Lorenzo, Phinehas, Joseph, and brother-in-law John P. Greene was almost a daily occurrence.

With his father being a resident of Kirtland and the Prophet Joseph Smith welcoming and always cordial, there were few things in Brigham's life amiss. Listening to the prophet preach truths of eternity and sitting in the same room with him at the School of the Prophets was a choice experience. Witnessing Joseph receive revelations from God to set in order the Church and Kingdom of God was priceless. It could be said that Brigham's situation was ideal. Yet he was lonely. In the gathering place of the Saints that had brought to his doorstep a crowd of family and friends, he was without female companionship.

150. Des Moines Daily News, October 16, 1886, p. 20, in Linda King Newell and Valeen Tippets Avery, Mormon Enigma: Emma Hale Smith (Garden City, NY: Doubleday & Company, 1984), p. 47.

"The Lord's Army Marching to the Delivery of Zion" from *The Rocky Mountain Saints* by T. B. H. Stenhouse, 1878. About 200 men and a number of women and children volunteered to join the expedition known as Zion's Camp.

Chapter Four

Zion's Camp

In spring of 1833 Brigham courted 30-year-old Mary Ann Angell. Mary Ann, the eldest daughter of James William Angell and Phoebe Ann Morton, was born June 8, 1803 in the town of Seneca in the Finger Lakes region of New York. She was reared to womanhood in Providence, Rhode Island, a hotbed of Quakerism.

Mary Ann was not drawn to the Quaker Society, but she did have religious leanings. She joined the Free Will Baptist Church and became a Sunday school teacher after studying Hebrew so that she could better understand the Bible. In 1831 she moved to the hamlet of China, New York to be near her younger brother, Truman O. Angell, a man who would one day be the famed architect of the Salt Lake Temple.

When Mary Ann arrived in the hamlet, she learned that Truman had accepted the Restoration message and entered baptismal waters. She was curious about her brother's new faith and his talk of Restoration. Given a Book of Mormon to read, Mary Ann read with great interest and concluded the book contained the word of God. Soon after, she met Brigham's brothers Joseph, Phinehas, and Lorenzo and brother-in-law John P. Greene. Each bore a strong testimony of the Restoration. Mary Ann believed their words and was baptized by John P. Greene. In obedience to the call to gather with the Saints of God, in 1832 she journeyed to Kirtland, Ohio.

Susa Young Gates wrote of Mary Ann Angell:

> Her study of the Scriptures, especially the prophecies, so engrossed her mind, that she confidently looked for their fulfillment, in consequence of which she resolved never to marry until she should meet a 'man of God,' one in whom she could confide and with whom her heart could unite in the active duties of a Christian life. Thus it was that she remained single until nearly thirty years of age.[151]

151. Gates, The Life Story of Brigham Young, p. 11.

152. Arrington, Brigham Young, American Moses, p. 37.

Mary Ann "felt drawn to him" as she listened to Brigham preach.[152] Brigham, likewise, was impressed with Mary Ann as he heard her bear testimony of Joseph Smith and the Book of Mormon. At age 32, Brigham married 30-year-old Mary Ann Angell on February 18, 1834 in Kirtland. Family tradition suggests that Sidney Rigdon officiated at their marriage.

Going from a single woman at age 30 to a married woman and a mother of two daughters was not without its struggles. Yet Brigham wrote that Mary Ann "took charge of my children, kept my house, and labored faithfully for the interest of my family and the kingdom."[153] The marriage of Brigham to Mary Ann was not one of convenience or mere respect. For those who question whether they loved each other, perhaps a postscript on a June 30, 1844 letter from Mary Ann to Brigham suggests the marriage was for love: "Life yours in haste if we meet no more in this world may we meet where parting is no more. Farewell, Mary Ann."[154]

153. Watson, Manuscript History of Brigham Young, p. 8.

154. Letter of Mary Ann Young to Brigham Young, June 30, 1844. Church History Library.

Fall of Zion

Four days after Brigham wed Mary Ann, Parley P. Pratt and Lyman Wight arrived in Kirtland on February

22, 1834 with distressing news. They brought detailed affirmation to the Prophet Joseph Smith of Saints being forced to abandon their homes in Jackson County and cross the Missouri River at the peril of their lives to reach safety in Clay County. They told of extreme suffering, persecution, and hostilities. Upon hearing their news, the Prophet Joseph cried, "Oh my brethren my brethren. . . . Oh! That I had been with you to have shared with you your trouble—My God My God what shall we [do] in such a case of trial."[155]

155. Lucy Mack Smith, History, 1844-1845, p. 8-9, bk. 13.

The next day February 23, 1834, Parley P. Pratt and Lyman Wight addressed the Saints assembled for Sunday services in Kirtland. They spoke of the suffering and hardships of Latter-day Saints in Jackson County. Brigham was in the assembly and listened to their report. He was anxious to learn details of what caused such extreme suffering and the number of Saints harmed.

What Brigham learned was that by fall of 1832, an estimated 1,200 Saints had organized themselves into small clusters throughout Jackson County. They built homes, shops, mills, ferries, bridges, and more. Church leaders Algernon Sidney Gilbert and William W. Phelps established a storehouse and a printing office. Construction of schools, even a school for the elders patterned after the School of the Prophets in Kirtland, was underway.

In what appeared prosperous circumstances, a mob element in Independence, a town whose name heralds man's inalienable rights, forced the Saints to abandon their property. The reason for such atrocities were unclear. It was assumed that fears of "old settlers" in Independence, sparked by economic competition and the outright threat of so many Northern non-slaveholders in town, led to hostilities. Brigham learned that Edward

Partridge had been coated with tar and feathers and "bore [his] abuse with so much resignation and meekness, that it appeared to astound the multitude, who permitted [him] to retire in silence, many looking very solemn, their sympathies having been touched."[156]

156. History, 1838-1856, volume A-1 [23 December 1805-30 August 1834], p. 327.

Brigham was told the meekness observed in Bishop Partridge went unnoticed by others as the mob continued its relentless attack on the Saints. "All my property was scattered to the four winds, tools and all for the pretended claims, where I owed not one cent justly," wrote Levi Hancock.[157]

157. Levi Hancock Autobiography, 1803-1882, typescript, p. 50. Church History Library.

Joseph Knight attempted to preserve his property from pillage and destruction but "submitted to the numerous indignities heaped upon [him] . . . [and he] made many concessions to the mob in the hope of pacifying them, but it was useless."[158] By November 1833 the Saints were fleeing from violence in Jackson County across the Missouri River to Clay County, where they hoped to find refuge and peace. Without adequate shelter and food, many exiles had become ill and others had succumbed to death.

158. Newell Knight, "Newell Knight's Journal," Classic Experiences and Adventures (Salt Lake City: Bookcraft, 1969), p. 97.

Brigham was still pondering what he had learned of the fall of Zion as the Kirtland High Council met on Monday, February 24, 1834 at the home of Joseph Smith to give audience to Parley P. Pratt and Lyman Wight. At the end of their graphic commentary on the lamentable circumstances of the exiled Saints of Jackson County, the Prophet Joseph declared that he was going to Missouri to redeem Zion and would ask for volunteers to go with him. He called upon the high council to sanction his decision, "which was given without a dissenting voice."[159] The Prophet was then nominated and seconded by the high council as the Commander-in-Chief of the Armies of Israel.

159. Kirtland Council Minute Book, p. 35. Joseph Smith Papers.

Later that same day, Joseph received a confirming

revelation from the Lord in support of his plans to redeem Zion:

> Verily I say unto you, my friends, behold, I will give unto you a revelation and commandment, that you may know how to act in the discharge of your duties concerning the salvation and redemption of your brethren, who have been scattered on the land of Zion. . . . I have decreed that your brethren which have been scattered shall return to the lands of their inheritance, and shall build up the waste places of Zion. . . . Let my servant Joseph Smith, Jun., say unto the strength of my house, my young men and the middle aged—Gather yourselves together unto the land of Zion, upon the land which I have bought with money that has been consecrated unto me (D&C 103:1, 11, 22).

The call to join Zion's Camp was issued six days after Brigham Young wed Mary Ann Angell. He was one of the first to express a willingness to join with Joseph Smith on his march to Missouri. Brigham wanted his brother Joseph Young to go as well but his brother was hesitant, knowing something of the inherent dangers entailed in the redemption of Zion. As Brigham and his brother were walking and discussing the march to Zion, Brigham recalled:

> We met the Prophet, who said to him, "Brother Joseph [Young], I want you to go with us up to Missouri." I informed the Prophet that my brother was doubtful as to his duty about going, to which the Prophet replied, "Brother Brigham and brother Joseph, if you will go with me in the camp to Missouri and keep my counsel, I promise you, in the

> name of the Almighty, that I will lead you there and back again, and not a hair of your heads shall be harmed," at which my brother Joseph presented his hand to the Prophet, as well as myself, to confirm the covenant.[160]

160. Watson, Manuscript History of Brigham Young, p. 8.

Volunteers for the Armies of Israel—Zion's Camp—were drawn from the greater Kirtland area and from Church branches throughout the middle and eastern states. It took over two months of recruiting before a sufficient number of volunteers and enough money had been gathered for the army to begin to take shape. In the evening of April 26, 1834, a priesthood meeting was held in the schoolhouse on the Isaac Morley farm.

Many recruits to Zion's Camp were in attendance. At the meeting, Joseph Smith invited the brethren to testify to the importance of the Restoration. After their remarks, the Prophet Joseph Smith arose and said:

> Brethren, I have been very much edified and instructed in your testimonies here tonight, but I want to say to you before the Lord, that you know no more concerning the destinies of this church and kingdom than a babe upon its mothers lap. You don't comprehend it.[161]

161. Wilford Woodruff Journal, as cited in James L. Bradley, Zion's Camp 1834: Prelude to the Civil War (Logan, UT: James L. Bradley, 1990), p. 25.

He concluded his remarks by prophesying of the future growth of the Church:

> It is only a little handful of the Priesthood you see here tonight, but this church will fill North and South America—it will fill the world. It will fill the Rocky Mountains. There will be tens of thousands of Latter-Day Saints who will be gathered in the Rocky Mountains, and there they will open the door

for establishing the gospel among the Lamanites. They will raise up a posterity there, and the Latter-Day Saints who dwell in these mountains will stand in the flesh until the coming of the Son of Man. The Son of Man will come to them while in the Rocky Mountains.[162]

162. Ibid.

The March to Zion

On May 5, 1834 Brigham Young bid farewell to his two daughters and his wife Mary Ann, who was pregnant with their first child. Brigham became one of 40 volunteers in Zion's Camp to leave Kirtland that day. Volunteers carried supplies with them for exiled Saints recently expelled from Jackson County. They also carried weapons in case Zion needed to be redeemed by force. According to family tradition, Brigham took with him "a good gun, a bayonet, a dirk, and powder and shot for protection. He also took an axe, a saw, a chisel, a spade, a hoe, and other garden tools."[163]

163. Young, Here is Brigham..., p. 91.

On their day of departure, the volunteers journeyed to New Portage, a distance of 53 miles. Brigham and Joseph Young spent the night at the home of Israel Barlow in New Portage. The next morning, they reported to camp with Israel Barlow by their side. Thus, one by one volunteers joined the camp increasing their number and their chances of victory.

Zion's Camp was composed of two divisions. The main division was led by the Prophet Joseph Smith, and a smaller division of 20 men from Pontiac, Michigan and northern Illinois was led by Hyrum Smith and Lyman Wight. The leaders of the two divisions prearranged a rendezvous at the Allred Settlement in Monroe County, Missouri and set a convergent course. Brigham Young and his brother Joseph were in the Joseph Smith division. This division was organized after a military pattern with the Commander-in-Chief, Joseph Smith, appointing general officers of the camp. Companies in the camp were composed of twelve men, each electing a captain from within its ranks. Brigham Young and Heber C. Kimball were elected captains of their respective companies. This was the first time either Brigham or Heber had been asked to preside over a group as large as twelve men. Captains were asked to follow standard camp procedure as they organized their groups of twelve—

> Two to attend to cooking, two to see that fires were made, two to pitch the tent at night and prepare the bedding and also to strike the tent each morning, two to fetch and provide water, one to do the running, two to see to the horses and wagon, and have everything prepared for starting. [The captain's] business was to see that the company was provided for, and that all things were done in order. [164]

164. Heber C. Kimball Autobiography, p. 21, in Arrington, Brigham Young, American Moses, p. 39.

Brigham was known in Zion's Camp for his singing, not for his leadership of twelve men. Brigham and his brother Joseph Young were accompanied by Levi Hancock on a fife made of a joint from an elder tree. "That fife," George A. Smith remembered, "may be considered almost the introduction of martial music among the 'Mormons.'"[165]

165. George A. Smith, "Historical Discourse," Journal of Discourses, 11:7.

In the evenings, Brigham and Joseph Young often sang duets. It was said, "[Their] musical voices cheered many a drooping heart, and encouraged their flagging energies while performing that memorable journey."

Levi Hancock wrote, "The songs of Brigham and Joseph were the sweetest I ever heard in the Camps of Zion."[166] A favorite anthem sung by the brothers was "Hark! Listen to the Trumpeters!"

166. Levi Hancock Journal, October 19, 1865, as quoted in Arrington, Brigham Young, American Moses, p. 40.

Hark! listen to the trumpeters!
They sound for volunteers;
On Zion's bright and flowery mount
Behold the officers.
Their horses white, their armor bright,
With courage bold they stand,
Enlisting soldiers for their king,
To march to Zion's land.

It sets my heart all in a flame
A soldier brave to be;
I will enlist, gird on my arms,
And fight for liberty.
We want no coward in our bands,
Who will our colors fly.
We call for valiant hearted men,
Who're not afraid to die.

To see our armies on parade,
How martial they appear!
All armed and dressed in uniform
They look like men of war.
They follow their great General,
The great Eternal Lamb;
His garments stained in his own blood,
King Jesus is his name.

The trumpets sound the armies shout,
They drive the host of hell,
How dreadful is our God, our King,
The great Emmanuel!
Sinners, enlist with Jesus Christ,

Th' eternal Son of God,
And march with us to Zion's land,
Beyond the swelling flood.[167]

167. "Hark! Listen to the Trumpeters!" text by George Careless.

As the camp traveled from Ohio to Missouri, the purpose of the camp was withheld from observers. Yet there was nothing that could stop questions or the curiosity of those who wondered why dozens of men were journeying together. For example, speculative reports of Zion's Camp reached Dayton, Ohio, before the men even entered the town.

Not knowing the destination of what some called the "Christian soldiers," anxiety ran high. About a dozen town leaders approached the camp to question the men. When asked where they were from, Brigham replied, "From every place but this, and we will soon be from this." When an enquirer asked, "Where are you going?" He answered, "To the West."[168]

168. History, 1838–1856, volume A-1 [23 December 1805–30 August 1834], p. 7.

When the camp halted its march on the Sabbath Day to hold worship services, residents of local towns came to observe. One such service was held at Jacksonville, Illinois on June 1, 1834, the 33rd birthday of Brigham Young. "This morning at half past 10 our trumpet, a common brass French horn, sounded in the Camp for preaching," wrote George A. Smith.[169]

169. History, 1838-1856, volume A-1 [23 December 1805-30 August 1834], p. 10 [addenda].

Approximately 300 residents from Jacksonville and the surrounding area gathered to listen to the service. The large attendance was attributed to Dr. Fredrick G. Williams, who had gone into the town the night before and informed the populous that there would be Sunday services the next morning in camp. Of that Sabbath Day meeting, George A. Smith penned,

When (Joseph Smith) took [the stand] professing to be a liberal free thinker he spoke to the people very freely about one hour on his particular views:

> He was listened to with great attention and those present remarked that he was one of the greatest reasoners they ever heard. The free thinker was followed by Elder John S. Carter, who delivered a very eloquent address on "Practical Piety." Elder Joseph Young spoke on the principles of free salvation, followed by Elder Brigham Young, who set forth baptism as necessary for salvation. . . . The congregation was also addressed by Elder Orson Hyde on baptism for the remission of sins.[170]

170. George A. Smith, "Memoirs," pp. 19-20, in Arrington, Brigham Young, American Moses, p. 41.

From this worship service, it appears that Brigham Young's standing before the Prophet Joseph Smith and among the brethren had risen, as he was now speaking during the same service with the prophet, instead of just listening to him. This was the first recorded instance of Joseph and Brigham preaching together. As the meeting concluded, residents of Jacksonville lingered, wanting to share their impressions of the preachers:

> They thought Joseph Young was a Methodist, and were anxious he should stay in the country and preach. They supposed Brigham Young was a close Communion Baptist, Orson Hyde a Campbellite or Reformed Baptist, Lyman E. Johnson a Presbyterian, Amasa Lyman a Restorationer and Orson Pratt a Unionist.[171]

171. Ibid.

Six days after the worship service at Jacksonville, the Joseph Smith division of Zion's Camp arrived at the Allred Settlement on June 7, 1834. The Hyrum Smith and Lyman Wight contingent arrived the following day. Lyman O. Littlefield wrote of Joseph greeting his brother Hyrum:

> The meeting with [Joseph] and his brother Hyrum was as might have been expected with two such noble men. [They were] united together by natural ties and with souls enlightened by divine influences, the fruits of which was to them the knowledge that God lived and communicated His will from the heavens to them as He had done anciently.[172]

172. Lyman O. Littlefield quote, in Jeffrey S. O'Driscoll, Hyrum Smith: A Life of Integrity (Salt Lake City: Deseret Book, 2003), p. 99.

At this point, Zion's Camp had a composition of 205 men under arms with a few women and children. They had not reached the number the Lord had asked for on February 24, 1834:

> It is my will that my servant Parley P. Pratt and my servant Lyman Wight should not return to the land of their brethren, until they have obtained companies to go up unto the land of Zion, by tens, or by twenties, or by fifties, or by an hundred until they have obtained to the number of five hundred of the strength of my house (D&C 103:30).

On June 17, 1834 the Prophet Joseph was apprised of a company of men preparing to attack the camp. "My brother Hyrum said he knew in the name of the Lord, that it was best to go on to the Prairie," Joseph wrote. "And as he was my Elder Brother I thought [it] best to heed his counsel, though some were murmuring in the Camp."[173] Hyrum "took the flag or standard . . . and gave the word to move forward, and the teams, immediately began to follow."[174] Because the Prophet Joseph heeded the Lord's inspiration to Hyrum to move the

173. History, 1838-1856, volume A-1 [23 December 1805-30 August 1834], p. 14 [addenda].

174. Minutes, 28-29 August 1834, p. 65. Joseph Smith Papers.

camp to the prairie, Zion's Camp was not attacked. Although not attacked by enemies on that occasion, the hardships of the fast marches proved difficult to endure. Joseph Young, in reflecting on his personal hardships on the march, said at a Zion's Camp reunion in 1865:

> I never went through a more severe trial of my faith; it was as much as we all could bear. We performed 100 miles in three days, in the hottest weather, some of us at times carrying our muskets and knapsacks weighing some 20 or 30 pounds on our backs, traveling until the blood could be heard in our boots and shoes.[175]

175. Deseret News, October 12, 1865, in Arrington, Brigham Young, American Moses, p. 40.

Brigham also spoke of extreme hardships and sickness in camp. He had compassion on those who suffered, but not for those who murmured:

> We performed a journey of two thousand miles on foot; we started on the 5th day of May, and accomplished that journey inside of three months, carrying our guns on our shoulders, doing our own cooking, etc. And instead of walking along without having to labor, much of the way we had to draw our baggage wagons through mud holes and over sections of bad road. Twenty or thirty men would take hold and draw a wagon up a hill, or through a mud hole; and it was seldom that I ever laid down to rest until eleven or twelve o'clock at night, and we always rose very early in the morning.
>
> I think the horn was blown at three o'clock to arouse us, to prepare breakfast, etc., and get an early start; and we averaged in the outward trip upwards of forty miles a day...[176] We laid on the ground every night, and there was scarcely a night that we could

176. Brigham Young, "The Handcart Emigration, etc.," Journal of Discourses, 4:101-102.

> sleep, for the air rose from the ground hot enough to suffocate us, and they supplied musketos [sic] in that country, as they did eggs, by the bushel.[177]

As days of marching extended to weeks, an attack of infectious cholera spread from man to man. "The brethren were so violently attacked that it seemed impossible to render them any assistance," wrote the Prophet Joseph. "The Heavens seemed sealed against us and every power that could render us any assistance shut within its gates."[178]

When Joseph tried to halt the spreading plague in the name of the Lord, he "learned by painful experience that when the Great Jehovah decrees destruction upon any people, and makes known His determination, man must not attempt to stay his hand."[179]

Sixty-eight men contracted cholera, and 13 die. Brigham and Joseph Young cared for the sick and helped bury the dead. "Their presence gave us much consolation," Heber C. Kimball said. Heber told of Luke Johnson being afflicted with cholera:

> While brother Luke Johnson was digging [a hole for a burial], the cholera attacked him with cramping and blindness; brother Brigham laid hold of him and pulled him out of the grave, and shook him about, talked to and prayed for him, and exhorted him to jump about and exercise himself; when it would leave him for a few moments, then it would attack him again; and thus we had the greatest difficulty to keep the destroyer from laying us low.[180]

Heber was also numbered among those afflicted with cholera and wrote of fighting "to extricate myself from the grasp of death."[181] Brigham and his brother Joseph

177. Brigham Young, "Temptation and Trials necessary to Exaltation," Journal of Discourses, 4:92.

178. Lucy Mack Smith, History, 1844-1845. Document Transcript, p. 12, bk. 13.

179. History, 1838-1856, volume A-1 [23 December 1805-30 August 1834], p. 505.

180. Heber C. Kimball, "Extract from the Journal of Heber C. Kimball," Millennial Star 26 (August 27, 1864), p. 551.

181. Ibid.

were not afflicted by cholera. As to how the cholera epidemic ended in camp, Brigham Young said:

> President Joseph Smith called the members of the camp of Zion together, and told them if they would humble themselves before the Lord, and covenant that they would from that time forth obey his counsel, that the plague should be stopped from that very hour, and there would not be another case in camp, whereupon the brethren with uplifted hands covenanted that they would from that very hour hearken to his counsel and obey his word, and the plague was stayed according to the words of the Lord through his servant.[182]

182. Ibid.

After the cholera epidemic passed, the Prophet Joseph took Brigham Young into his confidence. He confided in him that because of lack of unity and pride on the march, the men in Zion's Camp were not worthy in the sight of the Lord to enter Jackson County. The Lord affirmed in a revelation to the Prophet Joseph on June 22, 1834 near Fishing River, the unworthiness of the men in the camp. The Lord also revealed to the Prophet Joseph that the religious exiles of Jackson County had transgressed:

> Behold, I say unto you, were it not for the transgressions of my people, speaking concerning the church and not individuals, they might have been redeemed even now.
>
> But behold, they have not learned to be obedient to the things which I required at their hand, but are full of all manner of evil, and do not import of their substances, as becometh saints, to the poor and af-

> flicted among them. ...Therefore, in consequences of the transgressions of my people, it is expedient in me that mine elders should wait for a little season for the redemption of Zion—For behold, I do not require at their hands to fight the battles of Zion; for, as I said in a former commandment, even so will I fulfill—I will fight your battles (D&C 105: 2-3, 9, 14).

This was an extraordinary turn of events. The men of Zion's Camp had marched nearly 800 miles to redeem Zion and within a day of being in Zion, they were told to stop marching, for Zion would not be redeemed for a little season. They were also told that the reason for not redeeming Zion had as much to do with their actions as it did the exiles of Jackson County.

Unfortunately, few men in Zion's Camp recorded their feelings about this turn of events. No doubt Brigham was disappointed and perhaps a bit discouraged. Sadly, he did not pen of the lost opportunity to redeem Zion or of the failure to assist the Saints in getting back their lands in Jackson County.

Although the reaction of those who had marched toward Zion only to be rejected was not recorded, there are a few exceptions. For example, Luke Johnson, who had declared before leaving Kirtland that he would go to Jackson County or die in the attempt, took his brother Lyman and others to Jackson. He penned:

> We procured a boat and rowed over the Missouri River, landed in Jackson County, where we discharged three rounds of our small arms and immediately got into the boat with all our energies rowed back. Meanwhile the mob in Jackson County lined the shore [of the river] and commenced firing upon us, their balls skimming the water near us. After

> landing I returned fire and shot across the Missouri River.[183]

183. Luke Johnson Journal. Church History Library.

On July 3, 1834 the men of Zion's Camp were officially discharged by Lyman Wight as authorized by Joseph Smith. Wight gave the men a slip of paper certifying their military obligation had been fulfilled. The certificate given to Charles C. Rich reads:

> Liberty, Clay County, Missouri
>
> We hereby certify we are satisfied. [I]t is the duty of Brother Charles Rich to return to the east because of the Church and business. He is honorably discharged. July [3], 1834
>
> Signed Lyman Wight.[184]

184. Charles C. Rich Diary. Church History Library.

On Independence Day, July 4, 1834, Brigham and his brother Joseph, "in company with several of the brethren, started for home."[185] Brigham accepted the appointment as leader of a small group of brethren on the return journey. He wrote only one journal entry of his travels: "July 4, my brother Joseph and myself, in company with several (possibly eight) of the brethren started for home, and walked all the way, arriving in Kirtland in August."[186]

185. Salt Lake High Council Record, 1869-1872, pp. 83-84, in Arrington, Brigham Young, American Moses, p. 41.

186. Francis M. Gibbons, Brigham Young, Modern Moses/Prophet of God (Salt Lake City: Deseret Book, 1981), p. 38.

The Worth of Zion's Camp

Brigham was welcomed back into the loving arms of his wife Mary Ann and his daughters. For him, it was a joy to be home with his family. There was much he could now do to bless their lives. He improved their home, found woodworking jobs in town, and made time to labor again on the Kirtland Temple. The birth of his first son, Joseph Angell Young, was on October 14, 1834.

Although it appeared that family life had taken center stage, Brigham couldn't escape the nagging questions of why Zion's Camp had not succeeded. Brigham did not avoid naysayers who questioned the worth of the camp. He wanted to speak of the march and present his views even to critics.

While many viewed the camp a "failure," Brigham saw it of unquestionable value: "When I returned from that mission to Kirtland, a brother said to me, 'Brother Brigham, what have you gained by this journey?' I replied, 'Just what we went for; but I would not exchange the knowledge I have received this season for the whole of Geauga County; for property and mines of wealth are not to be compared to the worth of knowledge.'"[187]

187. Brigham Young, "The Gospel, etc.," Journal of Discourses, 2:10.

Of greatest value to Brigham was his uncompromising belief in Joseph Smith's prophetic calling which he attributed to the march to Missouri: "Since [then] we [Brigham and Heber C. Kimball] have never turned to the right or to the left. Neither of us was ever an enemy to Joseph Smith; we never pulled him back; we have always been ready to push him forwards; we never dictated to him in the first things, but we assisted him in carrying it out."[188]

188. Minutes of Young Family Meeting, Nauvoo, Illinois, 18 January 1845. Brigham Young Papers.

Brigham never questioned the value of Zion's Camp. To him, Zion's Camp was a life changer. Perhaps his most significant statement on the matter was made many years after the journey:

> I have travelled with Joseph a thousand miles, as he has led the Camp of Israel. I have watched him and observed every thing he said or did... I would not give the knowledge I got from Joseph from this Journey; and then you may take the State of Ohio

and the United States, and I would not give that knowledge for them. It has done me good and you good and this was the starting point of my knowing how to lead Israel. I watched every word and summed it up, and I knew just as well how to lead this kingdom as I know the way to my own house. It is God within me, and God upon me; God by day and by night, and it is for His Kingdom on the earth.[189]

189. Salt Lake High Council Record, 1869-1872, pp. 83-84, in Arrington, Brigham Young, American Moses, pp. 45-46.

A Private Meeting at Joseph's Home

About six months after Brigham had returned from Missouri and his attention had turned to his family and building the Kirtland Temple, he said, "My brother Joseph Young and myself had been singing after preaching in a meeting; and when the meeting was dismissed, Brother Joseph Smith said, 'Come, go down to my house with me.'"[190]

190. Brigham Young quote, in John A. Widtsoe, Discourses of Brigham Young, pp. 141-142.

This was on Sunday, February 8, 1835. Although Brigham had been brought into Joseph's confidence earlier in the School of the Prophets, and again in Zion's Camp, it was somewhat unusual for him to be called to a private meeting at Joseph's home.

Brigham wrote simply, "We went and sung to him a long time, and talked with him."[191] At that private meeting, Joseph told the Young brothers of a vision he had received of the men who died of cholera in Zion's Camp. He said, "Brethren,... if I get a mansion as bright as theirs, I ask no more." This was an astonishing statement. To tell the Young brothers of a vision that was not recorded in modern day scripture or by a scribe and then to know that the men who had died in the camp had received a mansion was truly remarkable. The mercy and kindness implied in the statement suggests that the

191. Ibid.

Prophet Joseph had continued to think of Zion's Camp much like Brigham, but in his case had a vision from God. After telling Brigham and Joseph Young of the vision, the prophet wept.

According to Joseph Young, "When [the Prophet] had relieved himself of his feelings, in describing the vision, he resumed the conversation" and told Brigham that he was one of the twelve special witnesses who would "open the door of the Gospel to foreign nations."

He told Brigham of the calling exactly one week before Brigham received his call to the Twelve. The Prophet Joseph then turned to Joseph Young and said, "Brother Joseph, the Lord has made you President of the Seventies."[192]

192. Joseph Young, History of the Organization of the Seventies (Salt Lake City: Deseret News, 1878), pp. 1-2.

Of Joseph Smith's prophetic announcements, Brigham said, "The subject of the Twelve and Seventies was discussed, it was the first time I ever thought of it." Although Brigham had read in the New Testament of Jesus calling Twelve Apostles and the Seventy and had preached much about the Restoration message, he had never contemplated that the Church would have apostles and seventies or that he would be called to such a high office.

The Prophet Joseph said, "Brethren, I am going to call out Twelve Apostles. I think we will get together, by-and-by, and select Twelve Apostles, (though it appears that Brigham had already been selected) and select a Quorum of Seventies from those who have been up to Zion."[193] The prophet instructed Brigham and Joseph Young to call a meeting the next Sunday of the brethren who had marched in the camp and had proven to the Lord their willingness to lay down their lives to redeem Zion.

193. Brigham Young, "Priesthood," Journal of Discourses, 9:89.

Joseph Smith, Brigham Young, and early Church leaders. From left to right: Hyrum Smith, Willard Richards, Joseph Smith, Orson Pratt, Parley P. Pratt, Orson Hyde, Heber C. Kimball, and Brigham Young. Painting by William W. Major about 1845.

Chapter Five
The Apostolic Call

Word spread quickly that a meeting was to be held on Saturday, February 14, 1835 at the newly constructed schoolhouse near the Kirtland Temple. Although the meeting was open to all Church members, the intent of the meeting was for "those who journeyed to Zion for the purpose of laying the foundation of its redemption."[194]

It had been over six months since the men of Zion's Camp had been discharged and encouraged to return to their loved ones. Since that time, most had been living in the greater Kirtland area and had become engaged in various activities. When asked why a meeting now, the answer was that the Prophet Joseph Smith intended to "appoint twelve special witnesses to open the door of the Gospel to foreign nations."[195] There was speculation as to who would be named as one of the special witnesses. Brigham Young was one of the names being circulated.[196]

194. Kirtland High Council Minutes, p. 147.

195. Joseph Young Sr., History of the Organization of the Seventies (Salt Lake City: Deseret News, 1878), pp. 1-2.

196. Kirtland High Council Minutes, p. 147.

The Call of the Twelve

The schoolhouse was crowded when Joseph Smith began the February 14, 1835 meeting. He opened the meeting by reading from the New Testament in the Book of John about the Lord's servants being chosen and ordained that "ye should go and bring forth fruit, and that your fruit should remain: that whatsoever ye shall ask of the Father in my name he may give it you" (John 15:16).

After the opening prayer, the Prophet Joseph spoke of having seen in vision those who had succumbed to cholera and death in Zion's Camp: "Brethren, I have seen those men who died of the cholera in the camp; and the Lord knows, if I get a mansion as bright as theirs, I ask no more."[197]

197. Joseph Smith, History of the Church of Jesus Christ of Latter-day Saints 7 vols. (Salt Lake City: Deseret Book, 1976), 2:181.

As he spoke of the vision, he wept and with difficulty told of another vision of the calling and order of the Twelve. Joseph then testified that it was the will of the God of Heaven that from men, who had left their families, homes, and shops to march with Zion's Camp to Missouri—men who were willing to lay down their lives to help the Saints forced to abandon their property in Jackson County—Twelve would be chosen.

Veterans of Zion's Camp were then invited to sit together. As others in attendance moved aside to make way for the veterans, the Prophet assured the assembly that it was the will of God that this meeting be held, for it was a meeting to ordain to the ministry men who had been tried like Father Abraham and proven themselves worthy. According to family biographer S. Dilworth Young, Joseph asked, "Did they agree? If so would all of the Zion's Camp men stand? All stood. A vote of the congregation to sustain this proposition was called for and a unanimous raising of the right hands followed."[198]

198. Young, Here is Brigham... p. 124.

The assembled were invited to join together to sing "Hark Listen to The Trumpeters!" the favorite song on the march to Zion, often sung by Brigham and his brother Joseph Young accompanied by Levi Hancock on the fife. Following their singing, Joseph Smith prayed and the meeting was adjourned for an hour.

As the meeting commenced an hour later, the Prophet Joseph announced the purpose of this meeting was so "the three witnesses of the Book of Mormon [could] pray each one and then proceed to choose twelve men from the church as Apostles to go to all nations, kindred, tongues and people."[199] The Three Witnesses—Martin Harris, Oliver Cowdery, and David Whitmer—stood up, prayed together, and were blessed by the laying on of hands by the First Presidency of the Church.

199. Minutes, Discourse, and Blessings, 14-15 February 1835, p. 149. Joseph Smith Papers.

Following the blessing, the Three Witnesses, "according to a former commandment, proceeded to make choice of the twelve." The "former commandment" was the June 1829 revelation in which the Lord told Oliver Cowdery and David Whitmer that they were called "even as unto Paul mine apostle, with that same calling with which he was called" (D&C 18:9). The revelation also specified the qualifications of the Twelve and commanded Oliver Cowdery and David Whitmer to "search out the Twelve," instructing them that "by their desires and their works you shall know them" (D&C 18:37–38).

The Three Witnesses proceeded to choose twelve men "as apostles, to go to all the nations, kindreds, tongues, and people."[200] According to historian Richard E. Turley, "The names had earlier been reviewed by Joseph Smith."[201] Those named as apostles of the Lord Jesus Christ were Lyman Johnson, Brigham Young, Heber C. Kimball, Orson Hyde, David W. Patten, Luke Johnson, William E. McLellin, John F. Boynton, Orson Pratt, William Smith, Thomas B. Marsh, and Parley P. Pratt. Three of the Twelve were not present at the schoolhouse—Thomas B. Marsh, William E. McLellin, and John F. Boynton. These men had not marched to Missouri in Zion's Camp.

200. Young, History of the Organization of the Seventies, p. 102; Minutes of the 10 October 1864 Reunion of Zion's Camp Veterans. Brigham Young Papers.

201. Richard E. Turley Jr., "The Calling of the Twelve Apostles and the Seventy in 1835," in W. Jeffrey Marsh, Joseph Smith and the Doctrinal Restoration (Provo, UT: Brigham Young University, 2005).

Lyman Johnson, Brigham Young, and Heber C. Kimball were invited to come to the front of the schoolhouse.

Before the congregation, each in his turn was ordained an apostle by the Three Witnesses. In his ordination and blessing, Brigham Young was promised—

> That he should be strong in Body, that he may go forth and gather the Elect preparatory to the great day of the coming of the Lord, and that he might be strong and mighty in declaring the tidings to nations that know not God, that he may add ten talents, that he may come to Zion with many sheaves.
>
> He shall go forth from land to land and from sea to sea, and shall behold Heavenly Messengers going forth, & his life shall be prolonged, and the Holy Priesthood is confirmed upon thee, that he may do wonders in the name of Jesus, that he may cast out Devils, heal the sick, raise the dead, open the eyes of the blind, go forth from land to land and from sea to sea, and that heathen nations shall even call him God himself, if he did not rebuke them.[202]

202. Blessing to Brigham Young, 14 February 1835. JS and others. Joseph Smith Papers.

The First Presidency affirmed the ordination and blessing of Brigham Young, Lyman Johnson, and Heber C. Kimball, then prophesied of "many things which should come to pass."[203] The meeting was then adjourned.

203. "Extracts from Heber C. Kimball's Journal," Times and Seasons, April 15, 1845, p. 868.

The Responsibilities of the Twelve

One week after the calling of the Twelve, on Saturday, February 21, 1835 the apostles met with the Prophet Joseph Smith. At this meeting, "Parley P. Pratt was called to the stand and ordained as one of the Twelve" by Joseph Smith, David Whitmer, and Oliver Cowdery. Following Pratt's ordination, Oliver Cowdery "called forwar[d] Orson Hyde, David W. Patten and Luke Johnson and proceeded to their ordination & blessing."[204] William E. McLellin, John F. Boynton, and William Smith were also ordained at the meeting. Although the blessings given to each apostle were unique, Heber C. Kimball summarized the blessings as—

204. Kirtland High Council Minute Book, p. 74.

> predict[ing] many things which should come to pass, that we should have power to heal the sick, cast out devils, raise the dead, give sight to the blind, have power to remove mountains, and all things should be subject to us through the name of Jesus Christ, and angels should minister unto us, and many more things too numerous to mention.[205]

205. "Extracts from H. C. Kimball's Journal," Times and Seasons, April 15, 1845, p. 868

According to Elder Kimball, after the February 21, 1835 meeting the Twelve "assembled from time to time as opportunity would permit, and received such instruction as the Lord would bestow upon us, and truly he blessed us with his spirit, and inspired his prophet to speak for our edification."[206]

206. Ibid.

For example, at a meeting on February 27, 1835, the Prophet Joseph posed the question, "What importance is there attached to the calling of these twelve apostles different from the other callings or offices of the church?"[207] After some discussion, Joseph answered his own query:

207. Minute Book 1, p. 88. Joseph Smith Papers.

> They are the twelve apostles who are called to a travelling high council to preside over all the churches of the saints among the Gentiles when there is no presidency established. They are to travel and preach among the Gentiles until the Lord shall command them to go to the Jews. They are to hold the keys of this ministry—to unlock the door of the kingdom of heaven unto all nations and preach the

> Gospel unto every creation. This is the virtue, power, and authority of their Apostleship—Amen.[208]

With this as their charge, within three weeks Joseph Smith again called the Twelve together for a meeting. At the March 12, 1835 meeting, the apostles were called as a quorum to go to the eastern states and were asked to leave on May 4, 1835. Believing themselves unprepared to leave Kirtland, the Twelve asked the Prophet Joseph to "inquire of God for us, and obtain a revelation, (if consistent) that our hearts may be comforted."[209]

The revelation received to comfort the Twelve is found in Doctrine and Covenants, Section 107. In this revelation, the Prophet Joseph was told:

> The twelve traveling councilors are called to be the Twelve Apostles, or special witnesses of the name of Christ in all the world—thus differing from other officers in the church in the duties of their calling. And they form a quorum, equal in authority and power to the three presidents previously mentioned.
>
> The Twelve are a Traveling Presiding High Council, to officiate in the name of the Lord, under the direction of the Presidency of the Church, agreeable to the institution of heaven; to build up the church, and regulate all the affairs of the same in all nations, first unto the Gentiles and secondly unto the Jews.
>
> The Twelve being sent out, holding the keys, to open the door by the proclamation of the gospel of Jesus Christ, and first unto the Gentiles and then unto the Jews (D&C 107:23-24, 33, 35).

At an April 1835 meeting of the Twelve, Oliver

208. Discourse, 27 February 1835—B, as Reported by William E. McLellin, p. 3. Joseph Smith Papers.

209. Minutes, 28 March 1835, Kirtland Record Book, p. 198. Church History Library.

Cowdery was assigned by Joseph Smith to speak on the great responsibilities that rest upon the Twelve. President Cowdery told the Twelve:

> You have enlisted in a cause that requires your whole attention... The greatness of your commission consists in this: you are to hold the keys of this ministry; you are to go to the nations afar off, nations that sit in darkness.

Cowdery spoke of faith expected of men called to be apostles of the Lord Jesus Christ: "You will see what you never expected to see; you will need the mind of Enoch or Elijah, and the faith of the brother of Jared; you must be prepared to walk by faith, however appalling the prospect to human view." He also spoke of their deliverance: "Your lives shall be in great jeopardy; but the promise of God is, that you shall be delivered."[210] Oliver Cowdery continued with instruction known as the "Apostolic Charge":

210. "History of Joseph Smith," Millennial Star 14 (April 2, 1853), pp. 209-212.

> If you in the least degree come short of your duty, great will be your condemnation; for the greater the calling the greater the transgression. I therefore warn you to cultivate great humility; for I know the pride of the human heart. Beware, lest the flatterers of the world lift you up... let your ministry be first. Remember, the souls of men are committed to your charge; and if you mind your calling, you shall always prosper...
>
> It is necessary that you receive a testimony from heaven, for yourselves; so that you can bear testimony to the truth of the Book of Mormon, and that you have seen the face of God. That is more than

the testimony of an angel. When the proper time arrives, you shall be able to bear this testimony to the world...

Never cease striving till you have seen God, face to face. Strengthen your faith; cast off your doubts, your sins, and all your unbelief...

With regard to superiority... God does not love you better or more than others... You are as one; you are equal in bearing the keys of the Kingdom to all nations... It is the will of your heavenly Father, that you proclaim His Gospel to the ends of the earth, and the islands of the sea.

Be zealous to save souls... bear this message to those who consider themselves wise: and such may persecute you; they may seek your life... be prepared at all times to make a sacrifice of your lives, should God require them in the advancement and building up of his cause. Murmur not at God. Be always prayerful; be always watchful...

We shall not see another day like this; the time has fully come, the voice of the Spirit has come, to set these men apart... It will require your whole souls, it will require courage like Enoch's. The time is near when you will be in the midst of congregations who will gnash their teeth upon you... did I say congregations would gnash their teeth at you? Yea, I say whole nations will gnash upon you; you will be considered the worst of men.

Be not discouraged at this. When God pours out His Spirit, the enemy will rage... the lives of those

> who proclaim the true Gospel will be in danger; this has been the case ever since the days of righteous Abel...
>
> Tarry at Kirtland until you are endowed with power from on High... The greatness of your commission consists in this:—you are to hold the keys of this ministry; you are to go to the nations afar off, nations that sit in darkness... You must prepare your minds to bid a long farewell to Kirtland, even till the great day come... You have a work to do that no other men can do; you must proclaim the Gospel in its simplicity and purity... all nations have a claim on you; you are bound together as the three witnesses were; you, not withstanding, can part and meet, and meet and part again, till your heads are silvered over with age.[211]

211. Ibid., pp. 211-212.

When Oliver Cowdery finished pronouncing the apostolic charge, he approached each apostle separately, taking each by the hand and asking, "Do you with full purpose of heart take part in this ministry, to proclaim the Gospel with all diligence, with these your brethren, according to the tenor and intent of the charge you have received?"[212] Each apostle answered in the affirmative.

212. Ibid., p. 212

Mission of the Twelve and the Chastisement of a Prophet

On Monday May 4, 1835, under the direction of Thomas B. Marsh, president of the Quorum of the Twelve, the apostles departed from Kirtland on their first and only mission as a full quorum. They journeyed to Fairport Harbor where they boarded the steamer Sandusky bound for Dunkirk, New York. They labored in the

Dunkirk area for a few days, preaching two-by-two before meeting at a previously arranged conference in Westfield, New York on May 9.

For five consecutive months members of the Twelve labored throughout New York, New England, and Upper Canada. They preached the Gospel of Jesus Christ, baptized, organized branches, and met periodically to confer and conduct business. Biographer Ronald K. Esplin wrote of their mission:

> In five months they covered hundreds of miles by wagon, canal boat, river steamer, railroad, stage, and foot. Traveling without purse or scrip, they experienced both friendship and rejection. They felt the power of God, and they felt they "had done as the Lord had commanded."[213]

When the Twelve returned to Kirtland, each found activities that required their attention. For Brigham Young, it was work on the Kirtland Temple. He labored alongside Artemus Millet, the stonemason he had baptized in Upper Canada. They placed stucco on the exterior of the temple. Brigham also worked with his brother Joseph Young on the "curved mullions and frames of the Gothic windows and the elliptical shapes in windows on the east and west facades."[214]

In recalling his labors and the labors of others, Brigham said—

> a mere handful of men, living on air, and a little hominy and milk, and often salt or no salt when milk could not be had; the great Prophet Joseph, in the stone quarry, quarrying rock with his own hands; and the few then in the Church, following his example of obedience and diligence wherever

213. "History of Heber C. Kimball," manuscript, in Ronald K. Esplin, "Brigham Young and the Transformation of the "First Quorum of the Twelve," in Susan Easton Black and Larry C. Porter, Lion of the Lord: Essays on the Life and Service of Brigham Young (Salt Lake City: Deseret Book, 1995), p. 59.

214. Richard Neitzel Holzapfel and R. Q. Shupe, Brigham Young: Images of a Mormon Prophet (Salt Lake City: Eagle Gate and Religious Studies Center, Brigham Young University, 2000), p. 14.

> most needed; with laborers on the walls, holding the sword in one hand to protect themselves from the mob, while they placed the stone and moved the trowel with the other.[215]

215. Brigham Young, "Necessity of Building Temples—The Endowment," Journal of Discourses, 2:31.

On the Sabbath, work on the Kirtland temple ceased. On that Holy Day, Brigham attended worship services, often preaching, singing, or serving at the sacrament table. All would have been well with Brigham had it not been for the long reach of Thomas B. Marsh and the jealousy, pettiness, and sparring among the Twelve.

Brigham smarted over being summoned by President Marsh to answer by what authority he had "presumed to appoint a meeting and preach" without consulting him. Brigham said of the leadership of President Marsh, it was "like a toad's hair comb[ing] up and down."[216]

216. Minutes, 12 February 1849. Church History Library.

The Prophet Joseph was aware of problems within the Twelve and the controlling leadership style of President Marsh. He wrote on November 3, 1835:

> Thus came the word of the Lord unto me concerning the Twelve saying behold they are under condemnation, because they have not been sufficiently humble in my sight, and in consequence of their covetous desires, in that they have not dealt equally with each other.

Offenders in the Twelve were named, but the Lord revealed "all must humble themselves before me, before they will be accounted worthy to receive an endowment."[217]

217. Joseph Smith Diary, 3 November 1835. Joseph Smith Papers.

The chastisement did not go unnoticed.

The Prophet Joseph wrote:

> Wm E. McLellen [McLellin] & Orson Hyde came in and desired to hear the revelation concerning the Twelve, when my scribe read to them they expressed some little dissatisfaction but after examining their own hearts, they acknowledged it to be the word of the Lord and said they were satisfied; after School Brig[h]am Young came in and desired also to hear, it... after hearing it he appeared perfectly satisfied.[218]

218. Journal 1835-1836, pp. 19-20, 5 November 1835. Joseph Smith Papers.

Brigham did not challenge the chastisement or question why. To him, it was the word of the Lord. From this point on, Brigham became a frequent invited guest in Joseph's home. His visits were never just social occasions. Each recorded visit had an element of instruction. For example, the Prophet Joseph wrote on December 16, 1835:

> Elder B[righam] Young and Elder J[ared] Carter called and paid me a visit, with which I was much gratified, I ex[h]ibited and explained the Egyptian Records to them, and explained many things to them concerning the dealings of God with the ancient[s] and the formation of the planetary System, they seemed much pleased.[219]

219. Journal, 1835-1836, p. 69, 16 December 1835.

A Holy Anointing

On the evening of January 12, 1836, all members of the Quorum of the Twelve Apostles were invited to meet with Joseph Smith in the Kirtland Temple to receive "the ordinance of holy anointing."[220] On that sacred occasion, the Prophet Joseph placed his hands

220. Joseph Smith Diary, 22-23 January 1836.

on the heads of each member of the Twelve and pronounced a blessing. Brigham wrote of that sacred experience, "I attended the solemn assembly, and, with my brethren of the Twelve, received my washings and anointings, and was privileged to listen to the teachings and administrations of the Prophet of God. We also attended to the washing of feet, which ordinance was administered to me by the Prophet Joseph."[221]

221. Watson, Manuscript History of Brigham Young, p. 13.

Nine days later on January 21, 1836, Joseph Smith wrote in his journal of a remarkable Vision which he saw of the Twelve and the Savior:

> I saw the Twelve Apostles of the Lamb, who are now upon the earth, who hold the keys of this last ministry, in foreign lands, standing together in a circle much fatigued, with their clothes tattered, and feet swollen, with their eyes cast downward, and Jesus standing in their midst, and they did not behold him. The Savior looked upon them and wept.[222]

222. Journal, 1835-1836, p. 137. Joseph Smith Papers.

Joseph went on to specifically write of Brigham Young:

> standing in a strange land, in the far south west, in a desert place, upon a rock... He was preaching to [twelve menacing men] in their own tongue, and the angel of God standing above his head, with a drawn sword in his hand protecting him, but he did not see it.
>
> And I finally saw the Twelve in the celestial kingdom of God. I also beheld the redemption of Zion, and many things which the tongue of man cannot describe in full.[223]

223. Journal, 1835-1836, p. 137-138, 21 January 1836.

Dedication of the Kirtland Temple

On March 27, 1836 the Kirtland Temple was dedicated. The dedication began with the singing of anthems—"Now Let Us Rejoice" and "The Spirit of God like a Fire is Burning." Sidney Rigdon offered the invocation. As he did so, "a glorious sensation passed through the House."[224] Hyrum Smith expressed gratitude for those who had sacrificed to build the temple, and asked the Lord to bless them. The dedicatory prayer, written under the direction of Joseph Smith, was then read by the prophet (see D&C 109).

In the prayer, Joseph asked the Lord to "let the anointing" of worthy brethren "be fulfilled upon them, as upon those on the day of Pentecost" (D&C 109:35-36). Joseph's petition was granted, for "the Savior made His appearance to some, while angels ministered to others, and it was a Pentecost and an endowment indeed, long to be remembered."[225]

Eliza R. Snow observed, "The ceremonies of that dedication may be rehearsed, but no mortal language can describe the heavenly manifestations of that memorable day."[226]

The highlight for many at the dedication was when the congregation arose to their feet and with hands lifted heavenward joined together in the Hosanna Shout: "Hosanna! Hosanna! Hosanna to God and the Lamb."

224. Truman O. Angell Autobiography, p. 5. Church History Library.

225. Journal, 1835-1836, p. 189. Joseph Smith Papers.

226. Edward Tullidge, Women of Mormondom (NY: Tullidge and Crandall, 1877), p. 95.

The shout was given three times, sealing the shout with Amen. Brigham then spoke in tongues. David W. Patten interpreted his words and also spoke in tongues. The Prophet Joseph stood and blessed the Saints. At about four in the afternoon, the seven-hour dedicatory service was over.

That evening, the Prophet Joseph and the Twelve and other Church leaders returned to the Kirtland Temple. After participating in the ordinance of washing of feet, Joseph spoke on the spirit of prophecy. Among other truths shared, Joseph taught, "[The Twelve] are not to serve tables, but to bear the keys of the kingdom to all nations. The Twelve are at liberty to go wheresoever they will and if one shall say, I wish to go to such a place, let all the rest say Amen."[227] As George A. Smith was speaking,

227. Joseph Smith Diary, 30 March 1836.

> A voice was heard like the sound of a rushing of a mighty wind which filled the Temple and all the congregation simultaneously arose being moved upon by an invisible power many began to speak in Tongues and prophecy others saw glorious visions; and I beheld the Temple was filled with angels which fact I declared to the congregation.
>
> The people in the neighborhood came running together (hearing an unusual sound within, and seeing a bright light like a pillar of Fire resting upon—the Temple) and were astonished at what was Transpiring... This continued until the meeting closed at 11 p.m.[228]

228. History, 1838-1856, volume B-1 [1 September 1834-2 November 1838], pp. 3-4 [addenda].

The Kirtland Temple dedication and the sacred events of that March 27, 1836 meeting marked the beginning of a Pentecostal season in the Church. One week later on April 3, 1836, other epochal manifestations were witnessed in the Kirtland Temple. Joseph wrote:

> Attended meeting in the Lord's House, assisted the other Presidents of the Church [the First Presidency and quorum presidents] in seating the congregation... In the afternoon, I assisted the other Presidents in distributing the elements of the Lord's Supper to the church, receiving them from the Twelve, whose privilege it was to officiate at the sacred desk this day. After having performed this service to my brethren, I retired to the pulpit, the veils being dropped, and bowed myself, with Oliver Cowdery, in solemn, but silent prayer.[229]

229. Journal, 1835-1836, pp. 191-192.

While in the act of prayer—

> the veil was taken from our minds, and the eyes of our understanding were opened. We saw the Lord standing upon the breastwork of the pulpit, before us; and under his feet was a paved work of pure gold, in color like amber. His eyes were as a flame of fire; the hair of his head was white like the pure snow; his countenance shone above the brightness of the sun; and his voice was as the sound of the rushing of great waters, even the voice of Jehovah (D&C 110:7).

The Savior said, "I have accepted this house. . . . And the fame of this house shall spread to foreign lands; and this is the beginning of the blessing which shall be poured out upon the heads of my people" (D&C 110:10).

When the vision closed, the heavens again were opened. Moses appeared and committed to Joseph

Smith and Oliver Cowdery "the keys of the gathering of Israel from the four parts of the earth, and the leading of the ten tribes from the land of the north."

Next came Elias, bestowing the keys of "the dispensation of the gospel of Abraham," which are the blessings and responsibilities of the Abrahamic covenant (see D&C 110:12; Abraham 2:9–11). And then "another great and glorious vision" was opened—Elijah appeared and bestowed the keys to turn "the hearts of the fathers to the children, and the children to the fathers" (D&C 110:13, 15).

Although these sacred events were rehearsed again and again over his lifetime, Brigham was not one to sit and ponder. He was an apostle of the Lord Jesus Christ. The word "apostle" means "one who is sent."

He was ready to "be sent" and anxious to return to the eastern states. He had a message to share—a message of a temple in Kirtland and keys restored. Knowing of his desire to serve another mission, Brigham was given an Elder's License "to preach the Gospel, agreeably to the authority of that office" signed by Joseph Smith.[230] The license reads:

> To Whom it May Concern
> This certifies that Brigham Young has been received into the Church of the Latter-day Saints, organized on the sixth of April, in the year of our Lord one thousand eight hundred and thirty, and has been ordained an Elder according to the rules and regulations of said Church, and is duly authorized to preach the Gospel, agreeably to the authority of that office.

230. License for Brigham Young, 30 March 1836. Joseph Smith Papers.

From the satisfactory evidence which we have of his good moral character, and his zeal for the cause of righteousness, and diligent desire to persuade men to forsake evil and embrace truth, we confidently recommend him to all candid and upright people as a worthy member of society.

We, therefore, in the name, and by the authority of this Church, grant unto this our worthy brother in the Lord, this letter of commendation as a proof of our fellowship and esteem; praying for his success and prosperity in our Redeemer's cause. . . .

Joseph Smith, Jun.

Chairman
F. G. Williams, Clerk
Kirtland, Ohio, March 30, 1836[231]

With license in-hand, Brigham left Kirtland for the eastern states. Of his eastward journey, he wrote:

> I had only traveled a short time to testify to the people, before I learned this one fact, that you might prove doctrine from the Bible till doomsday, and it would merely convince a people, but would not convert them. You might read the Bible from Genesis to Revelation and prove every iota that you advance, and that alone would have no converting influence upon the people. Nothing short of a testimony by the power of the Holy Ghost would bring light and knowledge to them—bring them in their hearts to repentance. Nothing short of that would ever do.[232]

231. "This certifies that the within license was recorded on the 30th day of March, 1836, in Kirtland, Ohio, in the License Records, Book A, page 5. Thomas Burdick. Recording Clerk. License for Brigham Young, 30 March 1836. Joseph Smith Papers.

232. Brigham Young, "Testimony of the Spirit—Revelation Given According to Requirements—Spiritual Warfare and Conquest, Etc.," Journal of Discourses, 5:327.

As Brigham journeyed from town to town, rejoicing in speaking of the Kirtland Temple and the restoration of priesthood keys from heavenly messengers, he was unaware that in his absence Kirtland was teaming with malcontents. Some within his own quorum were speaking of Joseph Smith as a fallen prophet.

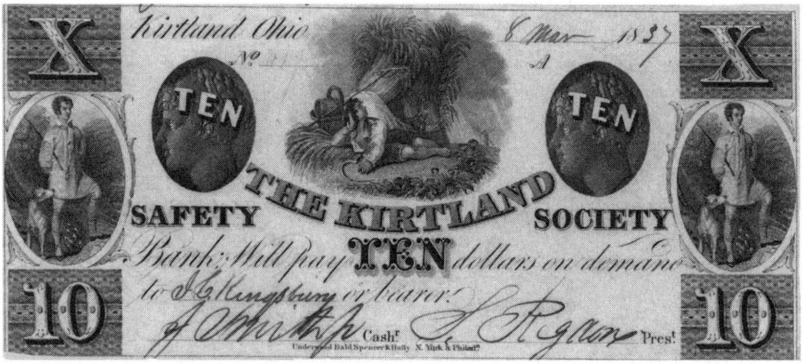

Ten Dollar bank note from the Kirtland Safety Society, made out to Joseph Kingsbury, dated 8 March 1837.

Chapter Six

Kirtland Safety Society

When the Kirtland Temple was under construction, Latter-day Saints willingly donated their time and means. Once the temple was completed and dedicated and the Pentecostal period had passed, financial contributions to the temple fund dried up. Outstanding bills went unpaid and lawsuits piled up against Joseph Smith for non-payment of debt.

On the one hand, Joseph was giving spiritual guidance and encouraging members to gather to Kirtland, and on the other hand, failing to meet the mounting pressure of financial obligations. The disparity between spiritual and temporal caused more than one Saint to question his leadership and his prophetic calling.

Seeking a solution to the mounting indebtedness, Church leaders gave serious consideration to establishing a bank. It was simple really—money placed in the bank could be used to pay down debt. Believing this would solve the financial problems and restore the faith of those who were wavering, on November 2, 1836 Church leaders drafted an "article of agreement" to organize the Kirtland Safety Society Bank.

Elder Orson Hyde was sent to Columbus, the capital of Ohio, with instructions to present the article of agreement to the state senate. As it turned out, his was not the only article of agreement requesting to charter a bank that was considered by the senate that year. Rather than consider each application on its merit, senators lumped the applications together as one bill or one article of agreement. As the bill was being discussed in the senate, Samuel Medary of Clermont County, Ohio, moved to amend the article by adding a section with the proviso: "The capital stock of which, shall be three hundred thousand dollars." A senate vote on the amended bill resulted in "Yeas 11, Nays 24."[233] The negative vote meant that the article of agreement to charter the Kirtland Safety Society Bank was denied.

Although denied the right to set up a bank, Church leaders were determined to go forward with organizing a financial institution to resolve the problem of indebtedness. On January 2, 1837, they established the Kirtland Safety Society Anti-Banking Company "for the promotion of our temporal interests, and for the better management of our different occupations, which consist in agriculture, mechanical arts, and merchandising."[234] Under the name of Joseph Smith, the following notice appeared in the Messenger and Advocate: "We invite the brethren from abroad, to call on us, and take stock in our Safety Society."[235]

Stock certificates were issued and "private land owned by the stock-holders along with what specie—gold and silver—that was received, became the capital basis" of the Kirtland Safety Society.[236] Unwittingly, this arrangement set the society up for failure because the land owned by the stockholders was mortgaged. Yet the 287 pages of the stock ledger book of the Kirtland Safety Society shows that 205 stockholders believed the company was on stable footing and were willing to put their monies in the Society.

233. Journal of the Senate of the State of Ohio, pp. 364-365.

234. Joseph Smith III, History of the Reorganized Church of Jesus Christ of Latter Day Saints 4 vols. (Independence: MO: 1896), 2:90.

235. "Articles of Agreement," Messenger and Advocate, January 1837, p. 443.

236. Max Parkin, "The Nature and Cause of Internal and External Conflict of the Mormons in Ohio between 1830 and 1838," Ph.D. dissertation, Brigham Young University, 1966, p. 167.

Failure of the Kirtland Safety Society

Less than a month after the Kirtland Safety Society was established, on January 31, 1837 the First Presidency of the Church journeyed to Monroe, Michigan to purchase "the charter of a bank there under which to operate and save the Kirtland enterprise." While the presidency was away from Kirtland, a plot to depose Joseph Smith was hatched. Although a meeting was held in the upper court of the Kirtland Temple for the purpose of appointing a new leader of the Church, little came of it.

What proved a greater red-herring was the attempt to redeem bank notes at face value in coinage. This led to the suspension of specie payment, meaning the Society would not exchange coins for paper money, even if the paper money was issued by the Society.

As the financial issue became a crisis, in February 1837 Joseph Smith and Sidney Rigdon were arrested and charged under an 1816 Ohio statute which prohibited the conducting of banking business save such was done by an authorized corporation.

A judge determined that Joseph Smith and Sidney Rigdon had operated the Kirtland Safety Anti-Banking Company as an illegal financial institution. Joseph and Sidney were found guilty of violating the 1816 statute and fined $1,000 each.

Difficult days followed for the Church and its leaders. Hoping to bring closure to the financial dilemma, Joseph and Sidney took a heavy stand against those who had means but refused to support the Kirtland Safety Society or recognize its currency. On April 9, 1837 Wilford Woodruff attended a meeting in the Kirtland Temple and reported on that Sabbath

Day, Joseph Smith

> Proclaimed that Severe Judgment awaited those Characters that professed to be his friends & friends to humanity & the Kirtland Safety Society But had turned traitors & opposed the currency & its friends... . Such have become Covenant Breakers for which they will feel the wrath of God.[237]

At the same meeting Sidney Rigdon said, "As many of the Church had refused Kirtlan[d] Currency which was their temporal salvation in consequence of this they put strength in the hands of their enemies & those that had done this thing must suffer by it."[238]

On May 10, 1837, after a nationwide run on the banks had taken at least a million in specie (coins) out of the vaults, New York City Banks suspended payments and closed their doors. Banks across the country followed suit in a domino effect. This led to a May 1837 national banking panic and the fall of the Kirtland Safety Society. Although there were many contributing factors to the failure, Joseph Smith, as treasurer of the society, was blamed for any and all financial losses.

Looking for a way out of the financial crisis and a way to acquire means to payoff subscribers and stockholders, Joseph Smith sent Brigham Young and his cousin Willard Richards to New York with instructions to raise funds from the Saints residing in small branches. Brigham and Willard were successful in baptizing and encouraging the Saints in New York to gather to Kirtland to see the magnificent temple built to the Most High God, but they were largely unsuccessful in collecting money.

Amid a firestorm of threats targeting Joseph Smith, the prophet remained relatively calm. He never lost

237. Scott Kenney, ed., Wilford Woodruff's Journals, 1833-1898 (Midvale, UT: Signature Books, 1983), 1:137-138.

238. Ibid.

sight of his prophetic role or the purpose of the Church. When it appeared there was little hope for the Church to retain a foothold in Kirtland, Joseph asked Heber C. Kimball to go without delay on a mission to England, promising him that his mission was for the "salvation" of the Church. Though Heber pled with the prophet for Brigham Young to accompany him, Joseph would not agree. Brigham was needed in Kirtland to speak in his behalf. Brigham urged Heber to go to England and promised him, "in the name of Israel's God you shall be blessed."[239]

239. Heber C. Kimball, "Faith and Works—Submission to Authority—The Lord's Provision for His Saints, etc.," Journal of Discourses, 6:65.

When word spread that Heber C. Kimball, Orson Hyde, and others were leaving Kirtland for England, Lyman Johnson chided Heber for being such a fool as to listen to "Joseph Smith, the fallen Prophet." Yet he gave him a cloak for the journey. On June 13, 1837 Heber and six others left Kirtland to share the message of the Restoration in the British Isles.

Painesville, Ohio

About six weeks later on July 27, 1837, Joseph Smith, Sidney Rigdon, and Thomas B. Marsh left Kirtland with plans to visit the Canadian Saints. They were accompanied by Brigham Young and Albert P. Rockwood, who acted more as guards than companions on the journey. Problems beset the traveling party when they reached Painesville, a distance of eleven miles from Kirtland. According to Brigham:

> When we arrived at Painesville, the Prophet was arrested by an officer for some pretended debt. Joseph immediately entered into trial before the court, which found no cause of action. After his release he was again arrested and brought before the court,

> when he was again dismissed. He was arrested the third time, and on examination was held over to trial. Brother Anson Call, who had lately joined the Church, stepped forward and proffered to become his bail.
>
> The Sheriff, who was personally acquainted with Anson Call, took him to one side and advised him strongly against being bail for the Prophet, asserting the Prophet would be sure to abscond, and he would lose his farm; but Brother Call willingly became his bail. On being released he was arrested a fourth time, for a debt of a few dollars, which was paid forthwith, and the fifth time he was arrested, which cause was soon disposed of, and he concluded to return to Kirtland for the night. As he got into his buggy, an officer also jumped in, and catching the lines with one hand, put his other hand on Joseph's shoulder and said, "Mr. Smith, you are my prisoner."
>
> Joseph inquired what was the cause of action. The officer informed him that a gentleman, a few months previous, had left a stove with him, for the price of which he was sued. Brother Joseph replied, "I never wished to purchase the stove, but the gentleman insisted on putting it up in my house, saying it would bring him custom." Joseph left his watch and other property in security.[240]

240. Young, Here is Brigham . . . , p. 166.

After spending the day in Painesville in six court cases, Joseph Smith and his traveling companions returned to Kirtland.

The next day, they started anew. This time "shunning Painesville and other places where we suspected our enemies were laying in wait to annoy Joseph." The traveling party spent the day in Ashtabula "wandering over the bluffs, through the woods and on the beach of the lake, bathing ourselves in her beautiful waters, until evening, when a steamboat arrived from the west." The party then boarded a steamboat and "took passage for Buffalo." That night Brigham "gave the Prophet my valise for a pillow, and I took his boots for mine, and we all laid down on the deck of the vessel for the night."[241]

241. Watson, Manuscript History of Brigham Young, p. 21.

Defending the Prophet

In the summer of 1837, "when temporal matters were talked of men were ready to decide at once, that they knew more than the Prophet about such matters." They did not doubt that Joseph had once "understood spiritual things that he understood the Spirit of the Lord, and how to build up a spiritual kingdom among men." But when it came to financial matters, he simply "did not understand anything about temporal" affairs.[242] As to where Brigham stood in the conversation, he said:

242. Brigham Young, "Confidence—Advice to Emigrants—Danger in Prosperity," Journal of Discourses, 1:74-75.

> I can tell the people that once in my life I felt a want of confidence in brother Joseph Smith, soon after I became acquainted with him. It was not concerning religious matters—it was not about his revelations—but it was in relation to his financiering—to his managing the temporal affairs which he undertook. A feeling came over me that Joseph was not right in his financial management, though I presume the feeling did not last sixty seconds, and perhaps not thirty. But that feeling came on me once and once only, from the time I first knew him to the day of his death. It gave me sorrow of heart, and I clearly saw and understood, by the spirit of revelation manifested to me, that if I was to harbor

> a thought in my heart that Joseph could be wrong in anything, I would begin to lose confidence in him, and that feeling would grow from step to step, and from one degree to another, until at last I would have the same lack of confidence in his being the mouthpiece for the Almighty, and I would be left, as brother Hooper observed, upon the brink of the precipice, ready to plunge into what we may call the gulf of infidelity, ready to believe neither in God nor His servants, and to say that there is no God, or, if there is, we do not know anything about Him; that we are here, and by and by shall go from here, and that is all we shall know. Such persons are like those whom the Apostle calls "As natural brute beasts, made to be taken and destroyed." Though I admitted in my feelings and knew all the time that Joseph was a human being and subject to err, still it was none of my business to look after his faults. . . . It was not for me to question whether Joseph was dictated by the Lord at all times and under all circumstances or not. I never had the feeling for one moment, to believe that any man or set of men or beings upon the face of the whole earth had anything to do with him, for he was superior to them all, and held keys of salvation over them. . . . It was not my prerogative to call him in question with regard to any act of his life. He was God's servant, and not mine.[243]

From this experience, Brigham learned to never let his mind tempt seeds of apostasy again or let his mind spiral downward with doubts about the Prophet Joseph. He also learned to steel himself against Satan's whispering attacks.

It was not that Brigham was unaware that Joseph,

243. Brigham Young, "He that Loveth Not His Brother Loveth Not God—If We Have Not Confidence in Our Leaders We Shall Not Have It in a Higher Power—The Church Holds the Keys of Salvation—The Providences of God to the Saints," Journal of Discourses, 4:297.

like other mortals, had faults, but Brigham knew that "it was none of my business to look after his faults." Joseph was in the hands of God. Brigham said, "It was not for me to question whether Joseph was dictated by the Lord at all times and under all circumstances or not."

The trap of apostasy that had ensnared other brethren, Brigham refused to accept. Critical words of those who tried to sway Brigham fell on deaf ears, for he knew that Joseph was "superior to them all, and held the keys of salvation over them." Had Brigham not thoroughly understood the place of the Prophet Joseph in the Lord's Kingdom, he never would have embraced or held on to "what is called 'Mormonism.[5]

Knowing that a conference of the Church was to be held in the Kirtland Temple on September 3, 1837 and that at the conference, a sustaining vote would be taken in support or rejection of Church leadership, Brigham was concerned. To him, the vote could go either way depending on whether the turncoats were organized.

"Owing to the disaffection existing in the hearts of many," Brigham said, "I went to the brethren whose votes could be relied on" to ask them to come to the temple "early in the morn'ing, and had them occupy the stand and prominent seats."[244]

> When the services began at 9 a.m., the first matter of business was sustaining of officers: Joseph and his first counsellor were received, his second counsellor; F. G. Williams, was laid over, not being present. The members of the Quorum of the Twelve in good standing, and the Authorities, generally, were sustained. We were also enabled to disfellowship those of the Twelve and others

244. Watson, Manuscript History of Brigham Young, p. 23.

245. Ibid.

> seeking to bring disunion and destruction upon the Church.[245]

Although a victory for the faithful in September 1837, two months later when the Kirtland Safety Society closed its doors, the scene was much different. Some 200 investors in the banking institution lost all or nearly all their money. How to reconcile their losses with the reasons for the bank's failure was not easy, especially when Joseph Smith had played such a key role. The issue of Church leadership was raised again—this time louder and organized.

Benjamin Johnson lamented how quickly the Saints were willing to consider their faith, cast aside the sacred, and succumb to organized apostasy:

> Men in high places began to complain of and reproach each other, and brotherly love was found smothered . . . all was now forgotten by many, who were like Judas, ready to sell or destroy the Prophet and his followers. And it almost seemed to me that the brightest stars in our firmament had fallen.[246]

246. Johnson, My Life's Review, pp. 20–21.

Turncoats denounced the presiding leaders as heretics, set up their own religious society, and took control of the Kirtland Temple. Brigham attended a meeting of the apostates in the temple where all around him men were accusing Joseph Smith of every manner of evil. Brigham had a difficult time being calm, for he was "pretty well charged with plenty of powder and ball" and "felt like a thousand lions:"[247]

247. Unpublished sermon of 8 October 1866, in Arrington, Brigham Young, American Moses, p. 57.

> [He] rose up, and in a plain and forcible manner told them that Joseph was a Prophet, and I knew it, and that they might rail and slander him as much as they pleased, they could not destroy the ap-

pointment of the Prophet of God, they could only destroy their own authority, cut the thread that bound them to the Prophet and to God and sink themselves to hell. Many were highly enraged at my decided opposition to their measures, and Jacob Bump (an old pugilist) was so exasperated that he could not be still. Some of the brethren near him put their hands on him, and requested him to be quiet; but he writhed and twisted his arms and body saying, "How can I keep my hands off that man?" I told him if he thought it would give him any relief he might lay them on... This was a crisis when earth and hell seemed leagued to overthrow the Prophet and Church of God. The knees of many of the strongest men in the Church faltered.[248]

248. Watson, Manuscript History of Brigham Young, pp. 16-17.

During what Joseph Smith called a "siege of darkness," Brigham said, "I stood close by Joseph, and with all the wisdom and power God bestowed upon me, put forth my utmost energies to sustain the servant of God, and unite the quorums of the Church."[249] He further said, "When I saw a man stand in the path before the Prophet to dictate him, I felt like hurling him out of the way and branding him as a fool."[250]

249. "History of Brigham Young," Millennial Star, August 1, 1863, 487.

250. Brigham Young, "Temporal and Spiritual Duties of the Saints, etc.," Journal of Discourses, 10:363.

Brigham Young, Joseph Smith, and Sidney Rigdon flee from Kirtland

On the morning of December 22, 1837, Brigham fled from the lawless in Kirtland. His public stance of claiming to know "by the power of the Holy Ghost that [Joseph Smith] was a prophet of the Most High God, that [he] had not transgressed and fallen as the apostates declared," made him a target for the unruly.

He wrote that his departure from Kirtland was the

251. History, 1838-1856, volume B-1 [1 September 1834-2 November 1838], p. 6 [addenda].

"consequence of the fury of the mob [and] the spirit that prevailed in the apostates."[251]

Brigham and his family journeyed about 150 miles from Kirtland to the agrarian community of Dublin, Illinois. They stayed in Dublin with Lorenzo Young. Brigham informed his brother Lorenzo that the Prophet Joseph Smith and others would soon be coming.

On January 12, 1838 Joseph Smith and Sidney Rigdon fled from creditors, apostates, and civil authorities in Kirtland, about three weeks behind Brigham's departure. A well-armed mob followed them for several miles. At one point, the mob spent the night in the same house where only a partition separated them from Joseph and Sidney. On another occasion, the mob passed Joseph and his family in a small Ohio village, but failed to recognize them.

Four days after leaving Kirtland, Joseph and his traveling party arrived in Dublin. There he met Brigham Young and other Saints who had anxiously awaited his arrival. They rejoiced together in the knowledge that all was well and they were free from persecution and bondage. Believing it wise to stay in Dublin for the winter, Joseph secured employment cutting and sawing wood. Brigham found calls for his woodworking skills. This was a choice time for the Prophet Joseph and Brigham—a time when their faith and confidence in the Lord Jesus Christ and his Latter-day work was joyous to contemplate.

On the Way to Far West

At the end of the winter season of 1838, Joseph wanted to push on to Far West, Missouri, but did not have sufficient means for the journey. He turned to Brigham. "Brother Brigham," Joseph said, "I am destitute of means to pursue my journey, and as you are one of the Twelve Apostles who hold the keys of the kingdom in all the world, I believe I shall throw myself upon you, and look to you for counsel in this case." Joseph wrote, "Brother Brigham thought I was not in earnest, but I told him I was."[252]

252. Young, Here is Brigham . . . , p. 183.

The humbleness of Joseph was revealed in this instance as he looked to Brigham—a man who had known much of poverty but now had sufficient means to continue the journey to Far West—for answers.

When Brigham realized the prophet's request was not in jest, he said to Joseph, "If you will take my council [sic], it will be, that you rest yourself, and be assured you shall have money plenty to pursue your journey."[253] Joseph wrote of how the money was procured to continue his journey to Far West:

253. History, 1838-1856, volume B-1 [1 September 1834-2 November 1838], p. 10 [addenda].

> There was a brother living in the place who had tried for some time to sell his farm but could not: he asked council [sic] of Brother Young concerning his property; brother Young told him that if he would do right, and obey council [sic], he should have an opportunity to sell. In about three days, Brother Tomlinson came to brother Brigham, and said he had an offer for his place; brother Brigham told him that was the hand of the Lord for to deliver brother Joseph Smith from his present necessity. Brother Brigham's promise was soon verified, and I got three hundred dollars from brother Tomlinson, which enabled me to pursue my journey.[254]

254. Ibid.

When Joseph Smith and his companions were about 200 miles outside of Far West, Brigham and his brother Lorenzo and their families caught up with them. They traveled together the rest of the way. Joseph wrote,

"They [Brigham and Lorenzo Young] were with us on the last of our journey which ad[d]ed much to our satisfaction."[255] Brigham mentioned only one incident on the journey:

255. Letter to the Presidency in Kirtland, 29 March 1838, p. 25. Joseph Smith Papers.

> One day while crossing a large Prairie, six or eight miles from any house, we crossed a small stream. The ground was frozen deep on each side, and we sprung one of the axle trees of Brother Barnard's carriage. Brother Barnard said we couldn't travel with it any farther. Brother Joseph looked at it and said, "I can spring that axle tree back so that we can go on our journey." Brother Barnard replied, "I am a blacksmith and used to work in all kinds of iron, and that axle tree is bent so far around that to undertake to straighten it would only break it." Brother Joseph said, "I'll try it." He got a pry and we sprung it back into place, and it didn't trouble us any more until we arrived at Far West March 14, 1838.[256]

256. Young, "Here is Brigham . . .," p. 184.

A photograph of Liberty Jail in Liberty, Missouri taken in 1896. Joseph Smith and five others were imprisoned here from December 1838 to April 1839. The jail had very primitive conditions—two very small windows, low ceilings, no bedding, and no protection from the cold.

Chapter Seven

Tribulations in Missouri

When Joseph Smith and his traveling party arrived in Far West, they saw "beautiful rolling prairies lay spread around like a sea of meadows . . . decorated with a growth of flowers that seemed as gorgeous [and] grand as the brilliance of stars in the heavens."[257]

In this picturesque setting, the weary travelers hoped the tribulations of Ohio were behind them. But tales of prejudice, hatred, and past wrongs from Saints in Far West sounded all too familiar—reminiscent of scenes in Ohio. Joseph knew there was much to accomplish before violence would again overtake them. He warned his followers to be alert and to protect themselves as they were living among "a ferocious set of mobbers, like lambs among wolves."[258]

257. History, 1838-1856, volume A-1 [3 December 1805-30 August 1834], p. 138.

258. Ibid., p. 213

He counseled the Saints to rise above retaliation for past and future wrongs and build up the communities of Far West and DeWitt in spite of looming outward challenges.

As for Brigham and his family, which consisted of his wife Mary Ann and children Eliza (age 13), Vilate (age 8), Joseph (age 4), and twins Mary Ann and Brigham Jr. (age 2), they settled near Mill Creek about eight miles east of Far West. Brigham built a log home, planted crops, and set up his woodworking shop. He hoped that this was a new day for the faithful—a day free from harassment and persecution—a day when the mob element was nowhere to be found.

But his hopes were in vain. Before long, the disaffected from Ohio arrived in Far West and "contaminated the minds of some of the brethren . . . against Joseph in order to destroy his influence."[259]

Surprisingly, Oliver Cowdery and David Whitmer listened and embraced their falsehoods. "Give me my freedom or take my life!" cried Cowdery. "I shall no longer be bound by the chains of hell. I shall speak out when I see a move to deceive the ignorant."[260] His cries were echoed by David Whitmer, who spoke of Joseph Smith "abandon[ing] the primitive faith" and "drift[ing] into error and spiritual blindness."[261]

The lies and false insinuations from once close friends did not alter the course of Joseph Smith. Not only did he continue to preach the word of God, he called upon the faithful to do the same. He spoke of plans to build a temple in Far West and establish a settlement at Adam-ondi-Ahman.

Brigham Young was supportive of Joseph's plans and left his farm labors and woodworking shop at Mill Creek to assist him in the governance of Far West. On April 6, 1838 Thomas B. Marsh, David W. Patten, and Brigham Young were "appointed Presidents Pro. Tem of the city of Far West."[262]

This meant that when the Far West High Council met five days later on April 13, 1838, these men presided. At that council meeting, charges against David Whitmer and Lyman Johnson were presented and discussed. Both men were excommunicated.

Four days later on April 17, 1838, the Prophet Joseph received a revelation freeing Brigham, for a little season, from further Church responsibilities:

> Revelation given to Brigham Young at Far West April 17th 1838. Verrily [sic] thus Saith the Lord,

259. Lucy Mack Smith History, 1844-1845, p. 10, bk. 14.

260. Huntington Library Letters, microfilm no. 87, in Stanley R. Gunn, Oliver Cowdery, Second Elder and Scribe (Salt Lake City: Bookcraft, 1962), p. 230.

261. David Whitmer, An Address to All Believers in Christ (Richmond, MO: 1887).

262. Journal, March-September 1838, 6 April 1838, p. 29. Joseph Smith Papers.

> Let my Servant Brigham Young go unto the place which he has bought on Mill Creek and there provide for his family until an effectual door is op[e] ned for the support of his family until I shall command [him] to go hence, and not to leave his family until they are amply provided for Amen.[263]

263. Journal, March-September 1838, Revelation for Brigham Young, 17 April 1838. Joseph Smith Papers.

There is no question that this revelation put Brigham out of the thick of profound matters. When others fought in the Battle of Crooked River or buried the dead at Hawn's Mill, the Lord wanted Brigham at home with his young family near Mill Creek. Was it because he had failed in his apostolic duties? It took Brigham a few months to discover the reason the Lord needed him at home.

The Extermination Order

Latter-day Saints, angered by years of threats and abuse, let their good sense of judgment fall to the wayside as they committed acts of violence that matched their foes. Tensions ran high between the Saints and old settlers and accusations went unchecked. Men reached for their weapons as women sought shelter.

The Battle of Crooked River brought the issue to a head. Believing government intervention necessary, turncoats sent an affidavit to Missouri Governor Lilburn W. Boggs claiming that Joseph Smith was a modern Mohammed and arming Indians with weapons. Although the affidavit was false, Governor Boggs acted upon the charges with a swiftness of executive power that surprised even the disaffected.

On October 27, 1838 he issued an extermination order: "The Mormons must be treated as enemies, and must be exterminated or driven from the State, if neces-

264. Correspondence from Governor Lilburn W. Boggs to Headquarters Militia, City of Jefferson, October 27, 1838, in History, 1838-1856, volume B-1 [1 September 1834-2 November 1838], p. 842.

265. Pratt, Autobiography of Parley Parker Pratt, p. 186.

266. Ibid., 187.

sary, for the public good, their outrages are beyond all description."[264]

The executive order put in harm's way every man, woman, and child who would not deny Joseph Smith was a prophet of God. The massacre at Hawn's Mill and the fall of DeWitt stemmed from the governmental decree. Fearful Latter-day Saints scattered, hoping to save their lives and find safety beyond the borders of Missouri.

Other Latter-day Saints hurried to Far West, hoping to find the town a bastion of safety. Instead, they found Far West encircled by militias bent on carrying out the governor's order.

On October 31, 1838 the Prophet Joseph and a handful of his closest associates, believing themselves with "no alternative but to put ourselves into the hands of such monsters, or to have the city attacked, and men, women and children massacred" ventured outside of Far West to speak with military leaders.

In so doing, they were betrayed. Parley P. Pratt wrote, "[We] commended ourselves to the Lord, and voluntarily surrendered as sheep into the hands of wolves."[265]

When news of their surrender passed from man to man in the militia, soldiers discarded military decorum and yelled like a lawless mob or as "so many bloodhounds let loose upon their prey." Parley penned:

> If the vision of the infernal regions could suddenly open to the mind, with thousands of malicious fiends, all clamoring . . . raging and foaming like a troubled sea, then could some idea be formed of the hell which we had entered.[266]

During the long evening hours, military guards

> Kept up a constant tirade of mockery, and the most

> obscene blackguardism and abuse. They blasphemed God; mocked Jesus Christ; swore the most dreadful oaths; taunted brother Joseph and others; demanded miracles; wanted signs, such as: "Come, Mr. Smith, show us an angel." "Give us one of your revelations." "Show us a miracle." . . . "Or, if you are Apostles or men of God, deliver yourselves, and then we will be Mormons."[267]

267. Ibid.

In answer to the mockery, Joseph and his associates fell silent. The danger they were in demanded their quiet attention.

A military tribunal—a court martial—convened to determine whether the Mormon prisoners should be permitted to live. General Alexander Doniphan stood in defense of the prisoners, arguing that the men "had never belonged to any lawful military organization and could not therefore have violated military law." He also spoke of the court martial as "illegal as hell."[268] In spite of his plausible arguments, the prisoners were condemned to death and General Doniphan ordered to carry out the execution.

268. Western Star, September 14, 1838, in Stephen C. LeSueur, The 1838 Mormon War in Missouri (Columbia, MO: University of Missouri Press, 1987), p. 48; see Sidney Rigdon Affidavit, July 1, 1843, Smith, History of the Church, 3:460.

> Sir: You will take Joseph Smith and the other prisoners into the public square of Far West, and shoot them at 9 o'clock to-morrow morning.
>
> Samuel D. Lucas
> Major-General Commanding

Doniphan replied to General Lucas:

> It is cold-blooded murder. I will not obey your order. My brigade shall march for Liberty tomorrow morning, at 8 o'clock; and if you execute these men, I will hold you responsible before an earthly

tribunal, so help me God!

A. W. Doniphan
Brigadier-General[269]

269. Smith, History of the Church, 3:190-191.

Privately, Doniphan told General Lucas:

> You hurt one of these men if you dare and I will hold you personally responsible for it, and at some other time you and I will meet again when in mortal combat and we will see who is the better man.[270]

270. Ibid.

The prisoners were not killed at Far West. Instead, General Lucas ordered that they be taken to Independence where they would be held in jail. One prisoner requested the right to gather food and clothing from his home in Far West for the journey ahead. Reluctantly, his request was granted which opened the way for all prisoners to return for necessities to Far West.

Prisoner wagons rolled through Far West at an early hour the next morning. When a wagon stopped in front of Joseph's home, a guard of six soldiers escorted him inside. "Father, is the mob going to kill you?" Joseph's young son asked. "You d--- little brat, go back, you will see your father no more," was a guard's retort.[271]

271. History, 1838-1856, volume D-1 [1 August 1842-1 July 1843], p. 1636.

After obtaining food and clothing, Joseph was forced back into the wagon and a tarp was pulled up over the wagon, preventing anyone from seeing him.

Among those who hurried to see him was his mother, Lucy Mack Smith. "Mr. Smith, your mother and sister are here and wish to shake hands with you," said a man standing near the wagon. "Joseph, do speak to your poor mother once more," cried his mother. "I cannot bear to go till I hear your voice." The words "God bless you, mother!" were spoken. The wagons then rolled out of Far West toward Independence.[272]

272. Lucy Mack Smith History, 1845, pp. 280-281.

Where was Brigham?

Where was Brigham when it appeared that Joseph Smith needed him most? Answer—eight miles away in Mill Creek fulfilling the revelation of the Lord to "provide for his family until an effectual door is op[e]ned for the support of his family until I shall command [him] to go hence, and not to leave his family until they are amply provided for."[273]

273. Journal, March-September 1838, Revelation for Brigham Young, 17 April 1838. Joseph Smith Papers.

Brigham was not at the Battle of Crooked River when David W. Patten was wounded. He was not at Hawn's Mill when the Saints were massacred and dead bodies were thrown down a well. He was not standing by Joseph when George Hinkle betrayed him.

But Brigham was aware of the horrific events that transpired. From his home on Mill Creek, he observed the approaching militia and wrote:

> At the time that the exterminating army of Governor Boggs, commanded by Generals Lucas and Clark, came in sight of Far West, I observed their approach, and thought that it might be the militia of the State which had come to the relief of the citizens; but to my great surprise I found that they were come to strengthen the hands of the mobs that were around us, and which immediately joined the army.[274]

274. Young, Here is Brigham . . . , p. 208.

When Brigham discovered that the militia had not come to relieve Latter-day Saints, he left Mill Creek and rushed to Far West. He wrote:

> I saw brothers Joseph Smith, Sidney Rigdon, Parley P. Pratt, Lyman Wight and George W. Robinson, delivered up by Colonel Hinckle to General Lucas, but expected they would have returned to the city

> that evening, or the next morning, according to agreement, and the pledge of the sacred honor of the officers that they should be allowed to do so, but they did not return at all.[275]

275. Ibid.

On November 1, 1838, Brigham observed the plundering of Far West:

> General [Samuel] Lucas demanded and took away the arms of the militia of Caldwell County... assuring them that they should be protected; but so soon as they obtained possession of the arms, they commenced their ravages by plundering the citizens of their bedding, clothing, money, wearing apparel, and everything of value they could lay their hands upon, and also attempting to violate the chastity of the women in sight of their husbands and friends, under the pretense of hunting for prisoners and arms. The soldiers shot down our oxen, cows, hogs and fowls, at our own doors, taking part away and leaving the rest to rot in the streets. The soldiers also turned their horses into our fields of corn.[276]

276. Ibidd.,, p. 209

Brigham heard the governor's proclamation read by General John B. Clark in Far West: "The Mormons must be treated as enemies, and must be exterminated or driven from the State, if necessary, for the public good, their outrages are beyond all description"[277]

Brigham heard General Clark say to an assembly of Saints:

277. Correspondence from Governor Lilburn W. Boggs to Headquarters Militia, City of Jefferson, October 27, 1838, in History, 1838-1856, volume B-1 [1 September 1834-2 November 1838], p. 842.

> The order of the Governor to me was, that you should be exterminated, and not allowed to remain in the State. And had not your leaders been given up, and the terms of the treaty complied with before

this time, your families would have been destroyed and your houses in ashes.

There is a discretionary power vested in my hands, which, considering your circumstances, I shall exercise for a season. You are indebted to me for this clemency. I do not say you shall go now, but you must not think of staying here another season, or of putting in crops; for the moment you do this, the citizens will be upon you; and if I am called here again in case of non-compliance with the treaty made, do not think that I shall act as I have done now. You need not expect any mercy, but extermination, for I am determined the Governor's order shall be executed.

As for your leaders, do not think, do not imagine for a moment, do not let it enter into your minds that they will be delivered and restored to you again, for their fate is fixed, the die is cast, their doom is sealed.

I am sorry, gentlemen, to see so many apparently intelligent men found in the situation that you are; and oh! if I could invoke that great Spirit of the unknown God to rest upon and deliver you from that awful chain of superstition, and liberate you from those fetters of fanaticism with which you are bound—that you no longer do homage to a man.

I would advise you to scatter abroad, and never again organize yourselves with Bishops, Priests, &c., lest you excite the jealousies of the people and subject yourselves to the same calamities that have now come upon you.[278]

278. Ibid.

Brigham later wrote that General Clark also said, "We must not be seen as many as five together. If you are, the citizens will be upon you and destroy you; but you should flee immediately out of the State. There is no alternative for you but to flee, you need not expect any redress; there is none for you."[279]

279. "History of Brigham Young," Millennial Star, August 29, 1863, p. 551.

Listening to the threats of General Clark, Brigham became extremely angry and thought to himself:

> "I will see you in hell first." Renounce my religion? "No, sir," said I, "it is my all, all I have on this earth. What is this world worth as it is now? Nothing. It is like a morning shadow; it is like the dew before the sun, like the grass before the scythe, or the flower before the pinching frosts of autumn. No, sir, I do not renounce my religion. I am looking beyond; my hope is beyond this vale of tears, and beyond the present life. I have another life to live, and it is eternal. The organization and intelligence God has given me are not to perish in nonentity; I have to live, and I calculate to take such a course that my life hereafter will be in a higher state of existence than the present.[280]

280. Brigham Young, "The Gospel—The Spirit of the Lord—Revelation," Journal of Discourses, 14:206.

Although stirred up with utter contempt for General Clark, the spirit whispered to Brigham to remain calm. Latter-day Saints needed him to be a beacon of strength to help them leave Missouri without further harm.

A Prisoner for Christ's Sake

In Independence, under the scrutiny of prison guards "hundreds flocked to see us day after day," wrote Parley P. Pratt. "We spent most of our time in preaching and conversation, explanatory of our doctrines and practice.

Much prejudice was removed, and the feelings of the populace began to be in our favor, notwithstanding their former wickedness and hatred."[281]

281. Pratt, Autobiography of Parley P. Pratt, p. 195.

From Independence, the prisoners were transported by guards to Richmond where they were shackled with irons. Joseph Smith wrote to his wife Emma:

> My Dear Emma, we are prisoners in chains, and under strong guards, for Christ['s] sake and for no other causes. . . . Brother Robinson is chained next to me he has a true heart and a firm mind, Brother Wight, is next, Br. Rigdon, next, Hyram, next, Parely, next Amasa, next, and thus we are bound together in chains as well as the cords of everlasting love, we are in good spirits and rejoice that we are counted worthy to be persecuted for Christ['s] sake.[282]

282. Letter to Emma Smith, 12 November 1838, p. 1. Joseph Smith Papers.

As Joseph and fellow prisoners waited for a court hearing to determine the cause for holding them in jail, they listened as unfeeling guards recounted atrocities committed in Far West. "I had listened till I became so disgusted, shocked, horrified, and so filled with the spirit of indignant justice that I could scarcely refrain from rising upon my feet and rebuking the guards," wrote Pratt. Joseph felt no such restraints.

> He stood erect in terrible majesty. Chained, and without a weapon; calm, unruffled and dignified [and] . . . spoke in a voice of thunder, or as the roaring lion. . . "SILENCE, ye fiends of the infernal pit. In the name of Jesus Christ I rebuke you, and command you to be still; I will not live another minute and hear such language. Cease such talk, or you or I die THIS INSTANT!"

The guards quailed before Joseph and "lowered or dropped" their weapons. Their "knees smote together, and who, shrinking into a corner, or crouching at his feet, begged his pardon, and remained quiet till a change of guards."[283]

283. Pratt, Autobiography of Parley P. Pratt, pp. 210-211.

Following this scene, a civil hearing was held at Richmond to determine if the state had just cause to keep the prisoners confined. As the courtroom filled to capacity, one man shouted, "There is a red hot Mormon, d-m him, I am acquainted with him." Another yelled, "Shoot your Mormon, I have shot mine."[284]

284. E. Robinson, "Items of Personal History," The Return, 2 (March 1890), pp. 16, 234, in LeSueur, 1838 Mormon War in Missouri, p. 198.

Judge Austin King failed to stop the outbursts. Witnesses swore to tell the truth but instead substantiated old rumors and fabricated new ones. Of their court testimonies, Joseph Smith wrote, "Renegade 'Mormon' dissenters are . . . spreading various foul and libelous reports against us thinking thereby to gain the friendship of the world." He concluded, "We have waded through an ocean of tribulation and mean abuse, practiced upon us by the ill-bred, and the ignorant."[285]

285. History, 1838-1856, volume C-1 [2 November 1838-31 July 1842], pp. 871-872.

As the hearing drew to a close, Judge King ordered Joseph Smith and five other prisoners to Liberty Jail on charges of overt treason. Outraged by the ruling, defense attorney Alexander Doniphan exclaimed, "If a cohort of angels were to come down, and declare [the prisoners] clear,... it would all be the same; for [King] had determined from the beginning to cast [them] into prison."[286]

286. Ibid., pp. 859-856.

On December 1, 1838 Joseph Smith and his associates were incarcerated in Liberty Jail. Two petitions requesting a writ of habeas corpus were denied. Why? Joseph believed it stemmed from hatred:

> The soldiers and officers of every kind hated us, and the most profane blasphemers and drunkards

& whoremongers hated us. They all hated us most cordially. And now what did they hate us for? purely because of the testimony of Jesus Christ.[287]

287. Ibid., p. 870

Latter-day Saints turn to Brigham Young

With the First Presidency held captive, David W. Patten killed at the Battle of Crooked River, and Thomas B. Marsh alienating himself from the faith, frightened Latter-day Saints looked to Brigham Young for guidance. Brigham, who had been a leader over twelve men in Zion's Camp and a supervisor of men painting on the Kirtland Temple, now faced thousands of frightened people looking to him for counsel. He staggered under the weight of the responsibility and inwardly questioned whether he was up to the task. However, he never doubted that the will of the Lord would prevail.

As the senior presiding leader in Far West, he took charge of administrative affairs. Brigham held meetings and made decisions without seeking counsel from others. For example, he presided at the Far West High Council on December 13, 1838: "When it was found that several were absent, who, (some of them) have had to flee for their lives, therefore it being necessary that those vacancies be filled the meeting was called for that purpose."[288]

At the meeting, Brigham "advised the councellors to be wise and judicious in all their movements and not hasty in their transactions; as for his faith it was the same as ever, and he fellowshipped all such as loved the gospel of our Lord and Savior Jesus Christ in act as well as word."[289]

It was not until January 16, 1839 that Brigham received a letter from the First Presidency—Joseph Smith, Sidney Rigdon, and Hyrum Smith—giving

288. Far West High Council Minutes, December 13, 1838, in Donald Q. Cannon and Lyndon W. Cook, Far West Record: Minutes of the Church of Jesus Christ of Latter-day Saints 1830-1844 (Salt Lake City: Deseret Book, 1983), p. 221.

289. Ibid.

specific directions on how he should proceed. The letter was addressed to:

> Bro H[eber] C Kimball and B[righam] Young
>
> Joseph Smith Jr Sidney Rigdon and Hyram [Hyrum] Smith prisoners for Jesus sake sends greeting.
>
> In obedience to your request in your letter we say to you as follows. It is not wisdom for you to go out of Caldwell with your Families yet for a little season until we are out of Prison after which time you may act your pleasure. But though you take your Families out of the state yet it will be necessary for you to Return and leave as before designed on the 26 of April.[290]

290. Letter to Heber C. Kimball and Brigham Young, 16 January 1839. Joseph Smith Papers.

The April 26 date was a reference to the revelation Joseph Smith received at Far West, five months previous on July 8, 1838:

> And next spring let them [the Quorum of the Twelve Apostles] depart to go over the great waters [Atlantic Ocean to England], and there promulgate my gospel, the fulness thereof, and bear record of my name.
>
> Let them take leave of my saints in the city of Far West, on the twenty-sixth day of April next, on the building spot of my house, saith the Lord (D&C 118:4-5). The First Presidency letter went on to explain the expected role of Brigham for a "little season":
>
> In as much as we are in prison and for a litt[l]e season if need be the management of the affairs of

the church devolves on you . . . the conversion of the world need not stop but under wise management can go on more rapidly than ever. . . .

If we live we live, and if we die for the testimony of Jesus we die, but whether we live or die let the work of God go on. . . . Brethren fear not, but be strong in the Lord and in the power of his might. What is man that the servant of God should fear him, or the son of man that he should tremble at him.

Neither think strang[e] concerning the fiery trials with which we are tried as though some strange thing had happened unto us. Remember that all have been partakers of like afflictions. Therefore rejoice in our afflictions by which you are perfected and through which the captain of our salvation was perfected also. Let your hearts and the hearts of all the saints be comforted with you, and let them rejoice exceedingly for great is our reward in heaven...

Brethren pray for us, and cease not, till our deliverance comes. which we hope may come. we hope we say, for our families sake.— Let the elders preach nothing but the first principles of the Gospel. and let them publish our afflictions. the injustice and cruelty thereof upon the house tops. Let them write it and publish it in all the papers where they go. charge them particularly on this point—

Brethren we remain yours in hope of Eternal life

Sidney Rigdon
Joseph Smith Jr.
Hyrum Smith[291]

291. Ibid.

After receiving the letter, Brigham and Heber C. Kimball went to Liberty to meet with the Prophet Joseph. On their visit, Joseph spent an hour talking with them, pausing only to ask Brigham how he felt about his calling. After returning to Far West, Brigham spoke at a public meeting about entering "into a Covenant to stand by, and assist each other to the utmost of our abilities in removing from this State."[292] The following covenant was then read:

292. History, 1838-1856, volume C-1 [2 November 1838-31 July 1842], p. 881.

> We, whose names are hereunder written, do for ourselves individually hereby covenant to stand by and assist one another, to the utmost of our abilities, in removing from this state in compliance with the authority of the state; and we do hereby acknowledge ourselves firmly bound to the extent of all our available property, to be disposed of by a committee who shall be appointed for the purpose of providing means for the removing from this state of the poor and destitute who shall be considered worthy, till there shall not be one left who desires to remove from the state: with this proviso, that no individual shall be deprived of the right of the disposal of his own property for the above purpose, or of having the control of it, or so much of it as shall be necessary for the removing of his own family, and to be entitled to the over-plus, after the work is effected; and furthermore, said committee shall give receipts for all property, and an account of the expenditure of the same.
>
> Far West, Missouri, January 29, 1839[293]

293. Young, Here is Brigham . . . , p. 212.

The number of Latter-day Saints who signed the

covenant at the meeting is unknown. By nightfall there were 80 signatures. The next day, Brigham secured 300 more, making in total 380 signatures.

The signed covenant signaled the exodus out of Missouri had begun. In the winter of 1839, thousands of religious exiles trekked nearly 200 miles from Far West to the banks of the Mississippi River. As Brigham saw the Saints pack their essential possessions in wagons and head down the road, he mused that this was not the first time Saints had been forced to leave their homes:

> We have, time and again, and again, been driven from our peaceful homes, and our women and children been obliged to exist on the prairies, in the forests, on the roads, and in tents, in the dead of winter, suffering all manner of hardships, even to death itself.[294]

294. Brigham Young quote, in Henry Asbury, Reminiscences of Quincy, Illinois: Containing Historical Events, Anecdotes, Matters Concerning Old Settlers and Old Times, Etc. (Quincy, Il: D. Wilcox & Sons, Printers, 1882), p. 161.

Photo of a frozen Mississippi River, late 1800s.

Chapter Eight

Quincy

On February 14, 1839, four years to the date that Brigham was ordained an Apostle of the Lord Jesus Christ at the schoolhouse near the Kirtland Temple, he took his leave of Far West. As the miles passed away under his feet, his determination to return to the City of the Saints two months later on April 26, 1839, did not lessen. Brigham was one of the multitude of Latter-day Saint exiles who journeyed to the banks of the Mississippi River. Most camped directly across from Quincy, Illinois—home to 1,600 settlers.

It was not the citizens of Quincy, the prosperous possibilities of the river-boat community, or the picturesque setting on the limestone bluff that led Saints to huddle on the riverbank. It was Brigham who counseled the Saints to head east to Quincy, for he knew ferry boats in the Quincy Bay could transport them away from Missouri to safety in Illinois.

Unfortunately, in the winter of 1839 floating ice prevented rivercrafts from conveying religious exiles to Illinois. The "ice had broken up on the west side of the river and was running so the ferry boat could not cross," wrote Sarah Rich. "All chance for crossing was to go across in a skiff or canoe through the ice until they reached the island and from there walk on the ice to reach Quincy on the east side."[295]

A few Saints attempted to cross the river in canoes, "paddling through the ice, the women holding onto the

295. Sarah Rich, Autobiography, pp. 29-30, L. Tom Perry Special Collections.

296. Jenson, Latter-day Saint Biographical Encyclopedia, 3:208.

side while the floating ice cut their fingers."[296] Most Latter-day Saint exiles were not willing to cross the treacherous waters.

During February and March of 1839, hundreds waited anxiously for the river to freeze and permit passage. From Quincy, Wandle Mace could see the huddled Saints across the river and wrote, "Some had sheets stretched to make a little shelter from the wind, but it was a poor protection, the children were shivering around a fire which the wind blew about so it done them very little good. The poor Saints here suffered terribly."[297]

297. Wandle Mace Autobiography, typescript, pp. 32-33. L. Tom Perry Special Collections.

One of the refugees waiting to cross the icy river was Lucy Mack Smith, who wrote:

> The snow was now six inches deep and still falling—we made our beds upon it and went to rest, with what comfort we might under such circumstances. The next morning our beds were covered with snow, and much of the bedding under which we lay, frozen. We rose and tried to light a fire; but finding it impossible, we resigned ourselves to our comfortless situation.[298]

298. Lucy Mack Smith, History, 1845, pp. 286-287.

As the river froze, Latter-day Saints crossed on the ice. Mosiah Hancock recalled:

> I being bare-footed and the ice so rough, I staggered all over. We finally got across, and we were so glad, for before we reached the other side, the river had started to swell and break up. Father said, "Run, Mosiah," and I did run! We all just made it on the opposite bank when the ice started to snap and pile up in great heaps, and the water broke through![299]

299. Mosiah Hancock Autobiography, p. 17. L. Tom Perry Special Collections.

Another who reached safety was Emma, the wife of Joseph Smith. With two babies (Alexander and Frederick) in her arms, and two children (Joseph and Julia) at her skirts, Emma walked across the frozen Mississippi. She wrote to Joseph in Liberty Jail, "No one but God knows the reflections of my mind and the feelings of my heart when I left our house and home, and almost all of every thing we possessed excepting our little Children, and took my journey out of the State of Missouri."[300]

300. Emma Smith Letter, 7 March 1839. Joseph Smith Papers.

Joseph replied with queries to the Lord: "O God, where art thou? And where is the pavilion that covereth thy hiding place? How long shall thy hand be stayed, and thine eye, yea thy pure eye, behold from the eternal heavens the wrongs of thy people and of thy servants, and thine ear be penetrated with their cries?" (D&C 121:1-2).

Quincy—A City of Refuge

Upon reaching the riverbank of Illinois, Latter-day Saints could not refrain from expressions of joy. Perhaps Parley P. Pratt best conveyed what the religious exiles felt: "[He] immediately stepped a few paces into the woods, and, kneeling down, kissed the ground as a land of liberty, and then poured out [his] soul in thanks to God."[301] He knew that he was now once more "free to seek the pursuits of happiness and the welfare of the human race."[302]

301. Pratt, Autobiography of Parley P. Pratt, p. 278.

302. Lyman Littlefield, Reminiscences (1888), p. 110. L. Tom Perry Special Collections.

For Brigham, his joy was tempered for he knew their lives were still in peril. Hate-filled Missourians were crossing the Mississippi River with the sole purpose of kidnapping unsuspecting brethren. Such was the fate of Alanson Brown, James Allred, Benjamin Boyce, and Noah Rogers who were forcefully taken from Quincy across the Mississippi River to Missouri.

Alanson Brown was hung from a tree until nearly strangled. Benjamin Boyce was tied to a tree, stripped of his clothing, and inhumanly beaten, as were Noah Rogers and James Allred.[303]

303. Wilford Whitaker, "The Life and Times of Benjamin Boyce: Farmer–Policeman (1812-1846)," in Daniel Boyce, Boyce Family History (Provo, UT: 1973).

Not wanting a similar fate for others, Brigham counseled the Saints to be mindful of their surroundings and to protect themselves if necessary. Citizens of Quincy offered protection, food, and clothing to the beleaguered Saints. Word of their kindness led other Saints to set their course for Quincy. So many Latter-day Saints arrived in Quincy in the winter of 1839 that they outnumbered Quincyans by more than three to one.

Advice to the Saints in Quincy

On March 17, 1839 a Church conference was held in Quincy. By a unanimous vote, Brigham served as chair of the conference. As such, he spoke to the assembled of—

> The circumstances of the Church at Far West, and his feelings in regard to the scattering of the brethren, believing it to be wisdom to unite together as much as possible, in extending the hand of charity for the relief of the poor, who were suffering under the hand of persecution in Missouri.[304]

304. History, 1838-1856, volume C-1 [2 November 1838-31 July 1842], pp. 898-899.

305. Ibid., p.899

Brigham admonished the Saints to organize in Church branches to nourish each other and to help each other "give heed to the revelations of God."[305]

The conference then transacted business. Among items of business was a unanimous vote to excommunicate George M. Hinkle, the man who betrayed the Prophet Joseph and other Church leaders into the hands of General Samuel Lucas outside of Far West. Also excommunicated were Frederick G. Williams, a member of the First Presidency of the Church, and Thomas B. Marsh, the first president of the Quorum of the Twelve Apostles. The conference then adjourned. George M. Hinkle, he never returned to Church fellowship. Frederick G. Williams, on April 6, 1840 he spoke to an assembly of Saints, humbly seeking forgiveness for his wrongdoing in Missouri and expressing his determination to do the will of God.

He was forgiven and received back into Church fellowship. For Thomas B. Marsh, it would take 18 years before he returned to fellowship. He asked a congregation of Saints on Temple Square in Salt Lake City on September 6, 1857, "I want your fellowship I want your God to be my God... I have learned to understand what David said when he exclaimed, "I would rather be a doorkeeper in the house of God than to dwell in the tents of wickedness."[306]

306. See Thomas B. Marsh, "Return of Thomas B. Marsh to the Church," Journal of Discourses, 5:208.

As the Saints spread beyond the barge community of Quincy to outlying areas, they followed Brigham's directive to organize themselves into small branches to care for each other and to help each other "give heed to the revelations of God."[307] Additional religious exiles were assimilated into the Church branches.

307. Ibid.

Yet, by April 1839, improvised tents still lined the riverbanks. "[I] saw a great many of the Saints, old and young, lying in the mud and water, in a rainstorm, without tent or covering," wrote Wilford Woodruff. "The sight filled my eyes with tears."[308]

308. "Wilford Woodruff History, from His Own Pen" Millennial Star, May 20, 1865, p. 311.

Wandle Mace, a New York Saint who had stopped in Quincy on his way to Missouri, offered his home as shelter: "Many nights the floors, upstairs and down, were covered with beds so closely it was impossible to set a foot anywhere without stepping upon someone's bed."[309]

309. Wandle Mace Autobiography, pp. 31-32.

The kindness of Wandle Mace was mirrored by other Quincyans. Lucy Mack Smith wrote of the "ladies of Quincy [sending] us every delicacy which the city afforded." Of special mention was the Messer family, of whom Lucy penned, "[They] sought every opportunity to oblige us while we remained in the place."[310]

Luman Shirtliff wrote of arriving in Quincy in the evening hours and "wondering how we should get up the hill with our things, as weak as we were, and where we could stay overnight." He then noted, "When the boat landed many of the citizens came on board" to assist.[311] Thus, in a very caring manner the citizens of Quincy assisted the exiled Saints.

But there was a downside. Quincyans found themselves financially burdened by their generosity. Wanting to do more than receive a handout, Brigham appointed his brother-in-law John P. Greene go east to raise additional "means to relieve the sufferings of this unfortunate people."[312]

Between the kindness of the Quincyans and the assertiveness of Brigham in sending his brother-in-law and others to raise funds to help the poor, Latter-day Saints were provided with needed sustenance to endure the winter.

310. Lucy Mack Smith, History, 1845, p. 289.

311. Luman Shurtliff Autobiography, p. 43, L. Tom Perry Special Collections.

312. Clark V. Johnson, ed., Mormon Redress Petitions: Documents of the 1833-1838 Missouri Conflict (Provo, UT: Religious Studies Center, Brigham Young University, 1992), p. 6.

The Twelve at the Far West Temple Site

On April 17, 1839, just one month after the first Church Conference in Quincy, Brigham called a council meeting of the Twelve. After sustaining George A. Smith as a member of the Twelve, Brigham led a discussion on the revelation given to Joseph Smith on July 8, 1838.

The revelation foretold of the Twelve departing for their mission to the British Isles from Far West on April 26, which was only nine days later. The question was—Should the Twelve fulfill the revelation? Biographer Leonard Arrington wrote, "[Some] considered the Lord would take the will for the deed and did not expect we would go to fulfill it."

But Brigham "felt differently." He asked for an expression by each member of the Twelve concerning the revelation. He listened to their reasoning before saying in a tone of finality, "The Lord God had spoken and it was our business to obey, and the Lord would take care of us." His demeanor and words were so filled with the spirit of the Lord that all present agreed to fulfill the revelation.[313]

313. Arrington, Brigham Young, American Moses, p. 71

But the next day, only six of the brethren crossed the Mississippi River and rode west from Quincy. Brigham Young, Orson Pratt, and Wilford Woodruff rode in one carriage. John Taylor, George A. Smith, and Alpheus Cutler in the other. They traveled fast, for they were on the Lord's errand and nothing could divert their journey. Surprisingly, although the revelation regarding the Twelve being at Far West on April 26th was known to the disaffected, there were no guards posted along the route to prevent their return to Far West.

It was as if the disaffected and the enemies of the Church were convinced the Twelve would not dare cross the Mississippi to travel 200 miles to fulfill prophecy. Little did they know the tenacity and determination of Brigham or others of the Twelve.

In the pre-dawn hours of April 26, 1839, Brigham stood on the Far West temple site and presided over a conference attended by the Twelve, high priests, elders, and priests. The first order of business was to excommunicate dissidents, most of whom were still living in Far West. A hymn was then sung. Alpheus Cutler, who had previously been appointed to construct the Far West Temple, laid the "foundation of the Lord's House, agreeably to revelation, by rolling up a large stone near the southeast corner" with the help of others.

The Twelve offered vocal prayers in the following order—Brigham Young, Heber C. Kimball, Orson

Pratt, John E. Page, John Taylor, Wilford Woodruff, and George A. Smith. They then sang "Adam-ondi-Ahman":

This earth was once a garden place,
With all her glories common
And men did live a holy race,
And worship Jesus face to face,
In Adam-ondi-Ahman
. . .
Hosanna to such days to come,
The Savior's second coming,
When all the earth in glorious bloom
Affords the Saints a holy home,
Like Adam-ondi-Ahman[314]

314. William W. Phelps, "Adam-ondi-Ahman," Hymns of The Church of Jesus Christ of Latter-day Saints (Salt Lake City: The Church of Jesus Christ of Latter-day Saints, 1985), p. 49.

After the singing, the Twelve departed from Far West, traveling across the state of Missouri to the Mississippi River. When they reached Quincy, the Prophet Joseph was waiting for them.

Joseph Smith arrives in Quincy

When hope seemed darkest in Liberty Jail, the Prophet Joseph wrote optimistic letters to Emma and the Saints in Quincy. To Emma, he penned, "As to yourself if you want to know how much I want to see you, examine your feelings, how much you want to see me, and judge for yourself, I would gladly walk from here to you barefoot, and bareheaded, and half naked, to see you and think it great pleasure, and never count it toil."[315]

315. Letter to Emma Smith, 4 April 1839, p. 2. Joseph Smith Papers.

To the Saints in Quincy, he wrote of his confidence in the Lord, "What power shall stay the heavens? As well might man stretch forth his puny arm to stop the Missouri river in its decreed course, or to turn it up stream, as to hinder the Almighty from pouring down knowledge from heaven upon the heads of the Latter-day Saints" (Doctrine and Covenants 121:33).

For himself and fellow captives, Joseph Smith wondered how much longer they must remain in captivity. In answer to his plea, the Lord assured Joseph:

> My son, peace be unto thy soul; thine adversity and thine afflictions shall be but a small moment; And then, if thou endure it well, God shall exalt thee on high; thou shalt triumph over all thy foes. Thy friends do stand by thee, and they shall hail thee again with warm hearts and friendly hands. Thou art not yet as Job; thy friends do not contend against thee, neither charge thee with transgression, as they did Job. . . . If the very jaws of hell shall gape open the mouth wide after thee, know thou, my son, that all these things shall give thee experience, and shall be for thy good. The Son of Man hath descended below them all. Art thou greater than he? . . . The ends of the earth shall inquire after thy name. . . . Fear not what man can do, for God shall be with you forever and ever (Doctrine and Covenants 121:7-10; 122:1, 7-9).

Their release from bondage can be traced to April 6, 1839 when Joseph Smith and fellow prisoners were taken from Liberty Jail in the custody of a strong guard assigned to transport them to Gallatin to answer the charge of treason.

On April 9 a formal hearing began in Gallatin before Judge Thomas C. Burch and a grand jury. At the conclusion of the hearing, the defense proposed that Judge Burch issue a change of venue for the prisoners. The judge agreed and ordered the prisoners be moved to Boone County.

The guards assigned to take the prisoners to Boone County, a hundred mile distance from Gallatin, were an escort of only five men. The prisoners left Gallatin on April 12 with the guards riding horses and the prisoners in a horse drawn wagon.

On April 16, the guards and prisoners arrived near Yellow Creek in Chariton County, Missouri. That night "the guards got intoxicated," wrote Joseph. "We thought it a favorable opportunity to make our escape... We took the advantage of the situation... and took our departure" for Quincy.[316]

316. Joseph Smith Jr., "Extract, from the Private Journal of Joseph Smith Jr.," Times and Seasons, November 1839, p. 7.

In the morning of April 22, 1839, Dimick B. Huntington was the first to see the Prophet Joseph in Quincy:

I Dimick Huntington saw Joseph land from the Quincy ferry boat about 8 [o'clock] in morning. He was drest in an old pair of boots full of holes, pants torn, tucked inside of boots, blue cloak with collar turned up, wide brim black hat, rim soped down, not been shaved for some time, looked pale & haggard:

> When I got within about 16 ft. of him he raised his head. I exclaimed My God is it you Bro. Joes. He raised his hand & stopped me saying Hush, Hush. He then asked where is my family. I told him they were 4 miles east at Judge Clevelands in a room I had provided for them. I asked him if he wished to see his father & mother as they were in Quincy. He said no it would be too great a shock, they are old & cannot bear it. Take me to my family as quick as you can.
>
> In passing through the back streets of Quincy a number of men knew him. On arriving at the house where his family was Emma knew him as he was

dismounting from his horse. She met him half way to the gate.[317]

317. Dimick B. Huntington, in David E. Miller and Della S. Miller, Nauvoo: The City of Joseph (Santa Barbara and Salt Lake City: Peregrine Smith, Inc., 1974), p. 26.

The Quincy Whig publicized the arrival of Joseph Smith:

> The celebrated Mormon leader, Joseph Smith, who has so long been in confinement in the upper part of Missouri, arrived in town on Monday last... We had supposed from the stories and statements we had read of "Jo Smith" (as he is termed in the papers) to find him a very illiterate, uncouth sort of a man; but from a long conversation, we acknowledge an agreeable disappointment. In conversation, he appears intelligent and candid, and divested of all malicious thought and feeling towards his relentless persecutors.[318]

318. Missouri Republican (St. Louis, MO), May 3, 1839, p. 2.

Joseph and Brigham in Quincy

Joseph had been in Quincy over a week before Brigham and the Twelve returned from Far West. As the prophet waited for their return, he witnessed "in our time of deep distress, [Quincyans] nobly came forward to our relief, and like the good Samaritan poured oil into our wounds, and contributed liberally to our necessities."[319]

319. Proclamation, 15 January 1841, p. 273. Joseph Smith Papers.

Whether it was food, clothing, shelter, employment or the hand of mercy, Quincyans did not hold back. They disregarded religious differences and embraced the downcast Saints as if they were family. They healed wounds, redressed wrongs, and offered hearth and home, sustenance, and their possessions to provide much-needed relief.

Wherever Joseph went, whether in the city of Quincy or outlying areas, he found kindness. On one of his short journeys with his brother Hyrum, they met

Brigham Young about four miles outside of Quincy. "It was one of the most joyful scenes of my life to once more strike hands with the Prophets, and behold them free from the hands of their enemies," Brigham wrote. "Joseph conversed with us like a man who had just escaped from a thousand oppressions, and was now free in the midst of his children."[320]

320. Watson, Manuscript History of Brigham Young, p. 40.

The chance meeting of Joseph and Brigham cannot be overstated. While Joseph had been away from the Saints locked in a loathsome prison, Brigham had carried out his instructions to the letter. The Saints were safe on the Illinois side of the Mississippi, the work of the Church was rolling forward, the Twelve had returned to Far West on the appointed date, and both men were now free in the cause of Christ. The meeting was emotional as the two stalwart friends embraced, knowing that each had a faith in God that had not been compromised by extremities.

The First Presidency, 1853. From left to right,
Heber C. Kimball, Brigham Young, Willard Richards.

Chapter Nine

The British Mission

In the 1830s, marshlands bordering the Mississippi River were touted as a bargain to unsuspecting investors in the eastern states. Speculator Isaac Galland saw the potential for a quick dollar in the infested swamp of Commerce on the Mississippi. But the financial panic of 1837 had dashed Galland's hopes.

Believing there was little potential for his investment gone sour, Galland offered to sell Commerce to the Latter-day Saints in exchange for valuable Missouri landholdings abandoned by them under the extermination order. The religious exiles from Missouri could afford little more and were enticed by his offer.

On April 24, 1839 the Prophet Joseph Smith "advised the brethren, who could do so, to go to Commerce and locate in Dr. Galland's neighborhood," which consisted of "one stone house, three frame houses and two block houses which constituted the whole city of Commerce."[321] About a week later on May 1, 1839, Joseph wrote:

321. History, 1838-1856, volume C-1 [2 November 1838-31 July 1842], p. 954.

> I this day purchased in connexion with others... a farm of Hugh White [in Commerce], consisting of one hundred and thirty five acres for the sum of five thousand dollars; also a farm of Dr. Isaac Galland, lying West of the White purchase for the sum of nine thousand dollars.[322]

322. Ibid., pp. 931-932.

On May 8 Joseph penned, "I was preparing to remove to Commerce, [and engaged in] counselling the brethren."[323] One day later, he and his family departed from Quincy, arriving in Commerce on May 10, 1839.

323. Ibid., p. 936.

"The place was literally a wilderness," said the Prophet Joseph of the swamplands in Commerce. "The land was mostly covered with trees and bushes, and much of it so wet that it was with the utmost difficulty a foot man could get through, and totally impassible for teams." He further observed, "Commerce was so unhealthy, very few could live there, but believing that it might become a healthy place, by the blessing of heaven to the Saints, and no more eligible place, presenting itself, I considered it wisdom to make an attempt to build up a City."[324]

324. Ibid., p. 954

The Prophet Joseph and his family resided in one of the blockhouses in Commerce, known as the Homestead. The two-story, 16' x 18' home located near the southwest corner of Main and Water streets was not only Joseph's first home near the bend of the Mississippi River but also Church headquarters. As for Saints living in Quincy and the outlying area, thousands packed up their possessions and followed Joseph to Commerce. They set up makeshift housing until other arrangements could be made.

Brigham Young, Orson Pratt, John Taylor, Wilford Woodruff, and Erastus Snow did not follow Joseph to Commerce. Instead, they took their families to an abandoned barrack across from Commerce on the west bank of the Mississippi River in Montrose, Iowa.

The barrack was part of Fort Des Moines No. 1, a military post from 1834 to 1837. When the post was abandoned in 1837, the army left commodious quarters that included a long barrack, stables, a hospital, and offices.

Joseph Meets Often with the Twelve

During what proved a busy May and June of 1839, Joseph Smith and his counselors took time to meet often with the Twelve, instructing them on doctrine and principles of leadership in anticipation of their forthcoming mission to the British Isles. At the June 3, 1839 meeting, Brigham was the first of the Twelve to receive a recommendation signed by the First Presidency to preach the gospel of Jesus Christ in Europe and in the nations of the world:

> To the Saints scattered abroad to the Nations of Europe and to the World—
>
> Be it known unto you that Elder Brigham Young is fully authourised to preach the gospel of Jesus Christ and his testimony can be relied on he is a man of unexceptionable character and received his authourity and Priesthood from under the hands of the Presiding authourities of the Church of Jesus Christ of Latter Day Saints who were called by actual revelation from God therefore God will bless him and bear record by his power thereby confirming his word and ministry thus testifieth your humble servants.—
>
> Sidney Rigdon
> Hyrum Smith
> Joseph Smith Jr[325]

325. Recommendation for Brigham Young, 3 June 1839. Joseph Smith Papers.

Few meetings were more impactful than the July 2, 1839 meeting at the Brigham Young home in the barrack on the west bank of the Mississippi. In attendance were the First Presidency, the Twelve and their wives, and members of the Quorums of the Seventy. The meeting began with singing and prayer, followed by instructions given to the "Twelve who were then about to take their departure on this most important mission, namely, to the Nations of the Earth and the Islands of the Sea."[326]

326. History, 1838-1856, volume C-1 [2 November 1838-31 July 1842], p. 963.

The First Presidency ordained Wilford Woodruff and George A. Smith to the Twelve and Theodore Turley to the Seventy. They blessed the "heads of the Wives of those about to go abroad."[327]

327. Ibid., p. 957.

As the meeting continued, Hyrum Smith spoke on the "necessity of their not trifling with their office, and of holding on strictly to the importance of their mission and the authority of the Priesthood."[328]

328. Ibid.

The Prophet Joseph admonished the "Twelve [to] be humble and not be exalted, and beware of pride, and not seek to excel one above another, but act for each other's good."[329]

329. Ibid., p. 9 [addenda].

He said, "That man who rises up to condemn others, finding fault with the church, saying that they are out of the way while he himself is righteous then know assuredly that that man is on the high road to apostasy."[330]

330. Ibid., p.10 [addenda].

The Miraculous Day of Healing

The month of July 1839 proved a particularly difficult time for the Saints living near the Mississippi. Weakened by their ordeals in Missouri and living in makeshift tents and wagons on the river banks, thousands of Saints fell prey to illnesses inherent in the Mississippi Valley.

Among the ill was Mother Smith. "I was taken very sick and was brought nigh unto death," she wrote. "For five nights Emma never left me, but stood at my bedside all the night long, at the end of which time she was overcome with fatigue and taken sick herself. Joseph then took her place and watched with me the five succeeding nights, as faithfully as Emma had done."[311] Joseph also fell ill with swamp fever.

331. Lucy Mack Smith, History of Joseph Smith by His Mother (Salt Lake City: Bookcraft, 1956), p. 319.

Brigham believed the reason for his illness was that he "had taken the sick into his house and dooryard until his house was like an hospital, and he had attended upon them until he was taken sick himself and confined to his bed several days."[332] A dramatic change to the prevailing sickness occurred on July 22, 1839. Wilford Woodruff wrote:

332. Journal, 1839, p. 9, editorial note. Joseph Smith Papers.

> [Joseph] arose from his bed and commenced to administer to the sick in his own house and door-yard, and he commanded them in the name of the Lord Jesus Christ to arise and be made whole; and the sick were healed upon every side of him. Many lay sick and dying along the bank of the river; Joseph walked along up to the lower stone house, occupied by Sidney Rigdon, and he healed all the sick that lay in his path... He called upon Elder Kimball and some others to accompany him across the river to visit the sick at Montrose...
>
> The first house he visited was that occupied by Elder Brigham Young... who lay sick. Joseph healed him, then [Brigham] arose and accompanied the Prophet on his visit to others who were in the same condition...
>
> The next place they visited was the home of Elijah Fordham, who was supposed to be about breathing his last... The Prophet of God walked up to the dying man and took hold of his right hand and spoke to him; but Brother Fordham was unable to

> speak, his eyes were set in his head like glass, and he seemed entirely unconscious of all around him... Joseph asked him if he had faith to be healed. He answered, "I fear it is too late; if you had come sooner I think I would have been healed."
>
> The Prophet said, "Do you believe in Jesus Christ?" He answered in a feeble voice, "I do." Joseph then stood erect, still holding his hand in silence several moments; then he spoke in a very loud voice, saying, "Brother Fordham, I command you, in the name of Jesus Christ, to arise from this bed and be made whole." ...It seemed as though the house shook to its very foundations. Brother Fordham arose from his bed, and was immediately made whole. His feet were bound in poultices which he kicked off; then putting on his clothes he ate a bowl of bread and milk and followed the Prophet into the street.[333]

333. Smith, History of Joseph Smith, p. 438.

Departure of the Twelve for England

On Sunday, August 4, 1839 Joseph wrote, "The Church came together for prayer meeting and Sacrament. I exhorted the Church at length, concerning the necessity of being righteous, and clean at heart before the Lord." Others spoke, including some of the Twelve, who "professed their willingness to proceed on their Mission... as soon as possible" and asked the Saints to "provide for their families during their absence."[334]

334. History, 1838-1856, volume C-1 [2 November 1838-31 July 1842], pp. 964-965.

From this point on, the Twelve prepared to leave their families. Wilford Woodruff wrote:

> As soon as any one of the Apostles began to prepare for starting he was smitten with chills and fever, or

> sickness of some kind. Nearly all of the quorum of the Twelve or their families began to be sick, so it still required the exercise of a good deal of faith and perseverance to start off on a mission.[335]

335. Mathias Cowley, Wilford Woodruff, His Life and Labors (Salt Lake City: Bookcraft, 1964), p. 108.

At what was believed to be the eve of their departure, the Twelve wrote an epistle to the Saints:

> The hearts of the Twelve are with you, and they, with you, are determined to fulfill their mission... They are now on the eve of their departure for England...They feel to pray for you, and to solicit an interest in your prayers... that God, may sustain them in their arduous undertaking; [and] grant them success in their Mission.[336]

336. History, 1838-1856, volume C-1 [2 November 1838-31 July 1842], pp. 960-961.

On August 8, 1839 John Taylor and Wilford Woodruff were the first of the Twelve to depart for the British Isles. Wilford, so weakened by illness, staggered from his home in the barracks down to the Mississippi.

Brigham assisted him into a canoe and paddled him across the river to Commerce. Wilford walked on his own to the post office before finding himself too weak to go any farther. When Joseph Smith saw him laying down outside the post office, he said, "Well, Brother Woodruff, you have started upon your mission." Wilford replied, "Yes, but I feel and look more like a subject for the dissecting room than a missionary." Joseph said, "What did you say that for? Get up, and go along, all will be right with you."[337]

337. Cowley, Wilford Woodruff, p. 109.

Twenty-one days after John Taylor and Wilford Woodruff departed, Parley P. Pratt and his brother Orson Pratt started on their mission. Others were delayed longer due to the sickness still prevalent in the swamplands. Leanora Taylor, the wife of Elder John Taylor, recalled carrying "several pails" of water to the household of Brigham Young in the barracks as he and his family were so ill they could not fetch "a drop" of water for themselves.[338]

338. Leonora Taylor to John Taylor, 9 September 1839, in Ronald K. Esplin, "Sickness and Faith, Nauvoo Letters," BYU Studies 15 (Summer 1975), pp. 427-431.

Yet on Saturday, September 14, 1839, just ten days after his wife Mary Ann had given birth to Roxy Emma Alice Young, Brigham left the barracks to begin his journey to England. He wrote of his departure:

> I started from Montrose on my mission to England. My health was so poor I was unable to go thirty rods to the river without assistance... I left my wife sick, with a babe only ten days old, and all my children sick and unable to wait upon each other.[339]

339. Watson, Manuscript History of Brigham Young, p. 50.

When his sister Fanny tried to convince him not to go, Brigham said to her, "Sister Fanny, I never felt better in my life." She replied, "You lie." Brigham did not reply. "I was determined to go to England or to die trying," he penned. "My firm resolve was that I would do what I was required to do in the Gospel of life and salvation, or I would die trying to do it."[340]

340. Deseret News Semi-Weekly, August 2, 1870, p. 1, in Teachings of Presidents of the Church: Brigham Young, p. 5.

After he crossed the Mississippi, Brigham got Israel Barlow to take him to the home of Heber C. Kimball. At Heber's home, Brigham went to bed. Three days later on September 17, 1839, Brigham's wife Mary Ann came across the river to comfort and care for him.

The next day, September 18, a wagon donated by Charles Hubbard, with a team driven by his son, drew up to the Kimball cabin. Brigham and Heber climbed into the wagon. With his wife Vilate and two of his children laid low with swamp fever, Heber said, "It seemed to me as though my very inmost parts would melt within me at the thought of leaving my family in such a condition."[341]

341. Kimball, "President Heber C. Kimball's Journal," p. 84, in James B. Allen, Ronald K. Esplin and David J. Whitaker, Men With a Mission, 1837-1841, the Quorum of the Twelve Apostles in the British Isles, (Salt Lake City: Deseret Book, 1992), p. 71.

He then told the young Hubbard boy to stop the wagon. Heber turned to Brigham and suggested that they stand and give a cheer to their loved ones. Helping each other to their feet, Brigham and Heber stood up in the wagon. They swung their hats over their heads three times, shouting, "Hurrah, hurrah, hurrah for Israel!" Their shout brought Mary Ann and Vilate to the doorway of the cabin. They called to their husbands, "Good bye; God bless you!"[342]

342. Ibid.

Journey across the States and to England

At the beginning of their eastward journey, Brigham and Heber had to stop often, being too feeble to continue. Yet nothing could stop them from fulfilling their mission to England. When they reached Pleasant Garden, Indiana, branch members gave them $8.50 to help defray their costs. This brought their combined financial resources to $13.50.

When they stopped in Kirtland, they found that they had paid over $87.00 in expenses out of the $13.50.[343] Brigham suspected that Heber had unknown resources, but such was not the case. Other miracles occurred along the way. Brigham wrote while crossing Lake Erie:

343. Watson, Manuscript History of Brigham Young, pp. 57-58.

> The lake was so rough that no boat came into port until the 26th, when we went on board the steamboat Columbus. . . . The wind rose about one o'clock in the morning. I went upon deck and felt impressed in spirit to pray to the Father, in the name of Jesus, for a forgiveness of my sins, and then I felt to command the winds to cease, and let us go safe on our journey. The winds abated, and I felt to give the glory and honor and praise to that God who

344. Ibid., pp. 58-59.

rules all things.[344]

On March 9, 1840, six months after they began their journey, Brigham Young, Heber Kimball, Parley and Orson Pratt, and George A. Smith boarded the Patrick Henry, a packet ship in the New York Harbor to sail to England. On the 28-day voyage, there were 16 days of storm and head winds.

The ship dropped anchor at the Liverpool dock on April 6, 1840, ten years to the date that the Church was organized and three years since Heber C. Kimball and Orson Hyde opened the work in England. Of their journey across the Atlantic and their landing in Liverpool, Brigham Young wrote. "I was sick nearly all the way and confined to my berth. . . . When I landed on the shore I gave a loud shout of Hosannah."[345]

345. Ibid., p. 69

Brigham and his brethren "soon found a room that we could have to ourselves, which made our solemn assembly glorious: we blest each other and prepared for our labor."[346]

346. History, 1838-1856, volume C-1 [2 November 1838-31 July 1842], p. 1049.

Publishing a Hymnbook in England

On Tuesday, April 14, 1840 the apostles held their first council meeting at the home of Willard Richards in Preston, England. (Willard had been living in England since he had accompanied Heber C. Kimball on his first mission to the British Isles three years before.) At the meeting, Brigham was sustained as president of the Twelve and Willard was ordained an apostle and received into the Quorum of the Twelve Apostles. The next day, a General Conference of the Church was held at the Temperance Hall in Preston.

Following the conference, Brigham sent a letter addressed to the "Saints of the United States," informing them that "the work of the Lord is progressing [in England]." He explained that since Orson Hyde and Heber C. Kimball had left England in 1838, "there have been about eight or nine hundred persons baptized.[347] He sent minutes of the General Conference and a personal letter to the First Presidency:

347. Smith, History of the Church, 4:115.

> To Pres't. Joseph Smith and counselors:
>
> Dear brethren, you no doubt will have the perusal of this letter, and minutes of our conferences; this will give you an idea of what we are doing in this country. If you see any thing in, or about the whole affair, that is not right: I ask, in the name of the Lord Jesus Christ, that you would make known unto us the mind of the Lord, and his will concerning us...
>
> Concerning the Hymn book, when we arrived here, we found the brethren had laid [aside] their old Hymn books, and they wanted new ones; for the bible, religion, and all is new to them. When I come to learn more about carrying books into the States, or bringing them here, I found the duties were so high that we never should want to bring books to the States. I request one favor of you, that is, a letter from you, that I may hear from my old friends. I trust that I will remain your friend through life, and in eternity.
>
> As ever,
> Brigham Young[348]

348. Letter from Brigham Young, 29 April 1840, pp. 121-122. Joseph Smith Papers.

The letter revealed not just Brigham's personal desire

to let the will of the Lord prevail, but his need for the approval of his actions by the First Presidency.

Sometime after receiving his letter, Joseph Smith told Mary Ann Young that he approved of all that Brigham had undertaken. Mary Ann wrote to Brigham, "J. Smith said he received nothing in [the] letter you had written that he disapproved of. But he wanted you to go ahead, be gloried in your resolutions to go ahead."[349] A few weeks later Brigham wrote to Joseph Smith. The subject was again that of printing:

349. Willard Richards to Brigham Young, August 22, 1840, in Allen, Esplin, and Whittaker, Men with a Mission, p. 135.

> Lugwardin[e] Herefordshire England
> May 7th. 1840
>
> Brother Joseph Smith
>
> Through the mercy of our heavenly Father I am alive and in pretty good health; better than I should have been had I remaind in America. . . .
>
> Shall we print the Book of Mormon in this Country immediately, they are calling for them for every quarter. The duties are so high on books, we need not think of bringing them from America; another question is the book of Doctrine and Covenants to be printed just as it is now to go to the nations of the earth, and shall we give it to them as quick as we can or what shall we do. Will the twelve have to be together to do business as a quorum, or shall they do business in the name of the church. Why I ask this is for my own satisfaction, if the Lord has a word for us, for one I am willing to receive it.

350. Letter from Brigham Young, 7 May 1840, pp. 150-153. Joseph Smith Papers.

Brigham Young[350]

While waiting for a reply, Brigham accompanied Wilford Woodruff to Manchester. There, he immersed himself in administrative affairs. Central to his work was printing news of the Restoration and raising funds for three publications—a hymnal, a periodical, and the English edition of the Book of Mormon. Of these publications, it was the hymnbook that led to a misunderstanding between Brigham and the Prophet Joseph Smith.

On October 27, 1839, five weeks after Brigham departed for England, the Nauvoo High Council "voted, that Sister Emma Smith select and publish a Hymn Book for the use of the Church, and that Brigham Young be informed of the same, and he not publish the Hymns taken by him from Commerce."[351]

Brigham did not receive word of the high council vote. He wrote to his wife Mary Ann in June 1840, "We are printing 3,000 copies of a hymn book."[352]

The British hymnal consisted of 78 of the 90 selections in Emma's 1835 hymnal and a 193 other hymns. As directed by the Nauvoo High Council, the second hymnbook that Emma compiled included 304 hymns with suggested tempos.

In November 1840 Brigham wrote to Mary Ann informing her of a letter he received from Joseph Smith after printing the English hymnal:

> In Brother Joseph's letter he sent to the twelve he said he had somethings against them, according to what I could learn about the letter it was because we did not [write] to him upon the subject of printing the hymnbook.[353]

351. "History of Joseph Smith," Millennial Star 17 (1855), p. 372.

352. "Letters of Brigham Young, 1836-1841," J. Willard Marriott Library; Letter of Brigham Young to Mary Ann Angel, June 12, 1840, Brigham Young Papers.

353. Letter of Brigham Young to Mary Ann Young, November 1840, in Newell and Avery, Mormon Enigma: Emma Hale Smith, p, 88.

On September 5, 1840 Brigham Young and Willard Richards wrote a twelve-page report to the First Presidency. Within the report, the question of the hymnbook again surfaced:

> Star office, 149. Oldham Road
> Manchester; Eng.
> Sept 5 1840
>
> To the first Presidency of the church of Jesus Christ of Latter Day Saints, viz, Joseph Smith Jun, Sidney Rigdon & Hyrum Smith,
>
> Beloved of the Lord and of his saints;
>
> According to council we have gatherd from different parts of England & Scotland, <a company of the> Breth[re]n, most of whom are very poor <and sisters> who are now in Live[r]pool ready to sail for America on Mo[n]day next.
>
> Most of them are very poor... We have heard by the bye that Brothers Joseph & Hyram Smith are coming to England next season...
>
> Shall we gather up all the saints we can & come over <with them> next Spring?
> Have we done right in Printing a hymn book?
>
> Your Breth[re]n in the Everlasti[n]g Cov
> B[righam] Young
> W. Richards[354]

354. Letter from Brigham Young and Willard Richards, 5 September 1840 pp. 1-12. Joseph Smith Papers.

Joseph Smith responded on December 15, 1840, addressing the issue of the hymnal and the importance of being in harmony with him:

Brother Brigham

I can assure you, that from the information I have received, I feel satisfied, that you have not been remiss in your duty but that your diligence and faithfulness have been such, as must secure you the smiles of that God, whose servant you are, and also the good will of the saints throughout the world.

The spread of truth throughout England is certainly pleasing; the contemplation of which, cannot but afford feelings of no ordinary kind in the bosoms of those who have had to bear the heat and burthen of the day.[355]

355. Letter to Quorum of the Twelve, 15 December 1840, p. 1. Joseph Smith Papers.

Joseph encouraged Brigham to move ahead with printing the Book of Mormon and the Doctrine and Covenants. He also expressed a confidence in the leadership of Brigham Young by saying, "There are many things of minor importance, on which you ask council, but which I think you will be perfectly able to decide upon as you are more conversant with the peculiar circumstances than I am.[356]

356. Ibid., p.2

Also on this date, Joseph Smith wrote to the Twelve of his gratitude for their untiring labors. Again the printing of the hymnals surfaced. This time Joseph expressed his approval:

Nauvoo Hancock Co, Ills.
Decr. 15. 1840

Beloved Brethren.

May Grace, Mercy, and Peace rest upon you, from

God the Father and the Lord Jesus Christ.
Be assured, my beloved brethren, that I am no disinterested observer of the things which are transpiring on the face of the whole earth and amidst the general movements which are in progress, none is of more importance, than the glorious work in which you are now engaged...

And I can assure you, that from the information I have received, I feel satisfied, that you have not been remiss, <in your duty> but that your diligence and faithfulness have been such, as must secure you the smiles of that God...

I have been favored by receiving a Hymn Book from you and as far as I have examined it I highly approve of it and think it to be a very valuable collection...

Give my kind love to all the brethren, and sisters, and tell them I should have been pleased to have come over to England to see them, but am afraid that I shall be under the necessity of remaining here for some time, therefore I give them a pressing invitation to come and see me.

I am D[ea]r Brethren Yours, Affectionately
Joseph Smith[357]

357. Letter to Quorum of the Twelve, 15 December 1840, pp. 1-8. Joseph Smith Papers.

A Reflection on his Year in England

In April 1841 Brigham was once again in Liverpool. It had been exactly one year since he first stepped on English shores.

This time, he was boarding a seafaring vessel to take him across the ocean to America. In a reflective mood, he penned of his twelve months in England:

> It truly seemed a miracle to look upon the contrast between our landing and departing from Liverpool.
>
> We landed in the spring of 1840, as strangers in a strange land, and penniless, but through the mercy of God we have gained many friends, established churches in almost every noted town and city in the kingdom of Great Britain, baptized between seven and eight thousand, printed 5000 Books of Mormon, 3000 Hymn Books, 2500 volumes of the Millennial Star, and 50,000 tracts, and emigrated to Zion 1000 souls, established a permanent shipping agency, which will be a great blessing to the Saints, and have left sown in the hearts of many thousands the seeds of eternal truth, which will bring forth fruit to the honor and glory of God, and yet we have lacked nothing to eat, drink or wear: in all these things I acknowledge the hand of God.[358]

358. Watson, Manuscript History of Brigham Young, pp. 96-97.

Daguerreotype of Nauvoo in the 1840s. About five months after the temple was completed, enemies of the Church burned out the inside. The temple was further damaged by a tornado in 1850. In February 1865, Nauvoo's city council ordered the final demolition of the last standing portion of the temple.

Chapter Ten

Nauvoo: A City Set Upon a Hill

The bustling city of Nauvoo was dramatically different from the Commerce that Brigham had left the year before. Saints were no longer huddled in makeshift shelters on the banks of the Mississippi, clinging to life as swamp fever took its toll. To thwart the spread of disease and to alleviate problems inherent in the marshy flatland, the Saints transformed the swamp by digging drainage ditches. Reverend George Peck observed them digging and noted with surprise:

> Some 200 miles above St. Louis, we saw on the Illinois side of the river a very singular encampment. A multitude of people, men, women, and children, ragged, dirty, and miserable generally, seemed to be living in tents and covered wagons for lack of better habitations. This strange scene presented itself along the shore for a mile or more. We were informed that they were Mormons.[359]

359. George Peck, The Life and Times of Rev. George Peck, D.D., written by Himself (NY: Nelson and Phillips, 1874), pp. 201-202.

Although disheartened by the herculean effort required to drain the swamp, the Saints did not quit. As the Prophet Joseph Smith observed their tenacity, he renamed the village of Commerce, Nauvoo, a Hebrew word meaning "a beautiful place or situation." Joseph foresaw the day when Nauvoo would rise from the remnants of the swamp and become a beacon, a "light of the world—a city set upon a hill."[360]

360. Heber J. Grant, in Conference Report, April 1900, p. 21.

To build such a city, the Saints had tackled their makeshift housing problem with the same zeal that characterized their efforts to reclaim the swamp. With hammer, saw, trowel, and shovel, they replaced the squalor of tents and log cabins with permanent structures.

The sights and sounds of permanence in Nauvoo were of epic proportions to passersby. "Nauvoo grew, with magic rapidity, from a few rude homes to a magnificent city," wrote Harvey Cluff. "Houses increased in number, farms were opened up and prairie lands east of the city converted into prosperous fields of golden grain."[361] To John Butler, "Everyone was building and you could look over the little settlement and see the hand of industry in every corner."[362]

361. Harvey Cluff Autobiography, typescript, pp. 4-5. L. Tom Perry Special Collections.

362. John L. Butler Autobiography, p. 23. Church History Library.

The Saints transformation of an undesirable swamp into a thriving community was observed by Colonel Thomas L. Kane:

> A beautiful city lay glittering in the fresh morning sun... The city appeared to cover several miles, and beyond it, in the background, there rolled off a fair country, checkered by the careful lines of fruitful husbandry. The unmistakable markers of industry, enterprise, and educated wealth everywhere, made the scene one of singular and most striking beauty.[363]

363. Thomas L. Kane, The Mormons: A Discourse Delivered before the Historical Society of Pennsylvania: March 26, 1850 (Philadelphia: King & Baird, 1850), pp. 3-5.

Home and shop next to barn and stable, with a family garden in between, had become the norm. Yet there was nothing normal about the growth of Nauvoo. The meandering Mississippi was in sharp contrast to the grist mills, lumber mills, potteries, tanneries, brickyards, bakeries, and dozens of home industries that had sprung up all around.

In July 1841 returning missionary Heber C. Kimball wrote, "When we got in sight of Nauvoo [coming up the

Mississippi by riverboat] we were surprised to see what improvements had been made since we left home. You know there were not more than thirty buildings in the city when we left . . . but at this time there are 1200; and hundreds of others in progress which will be finished."[364]

364. B. H. Roberts, A Comprehensive History of the Church of Jesus Christ of Latter-day Saints 6 vols. (Provo, UT: Brigham Young University Press, 1965), 2:84.

Brigham did not record his reaction to seeing the city of Nauvoo. What was on his mind and heart was Mary Ann and his children—little Emma, his twins Brigham and Mary Ann, his son Joseph, and his oldest daughters Vilate and Elizabeth. In his absence, he had prayed for their welfare, but now he could hold them in his arms. He wrote of them:

> I found my family living in a small unfinished log cabin situated on a low, wet lot [in Nauvoo], so swampy that when the first attempt was made to plow it the oxen mired; but after the city was drained it became a very valuable garden spot.
>
> Although I had to spend the principal part of my time, at the call of Brother Joseph, in the service of the Church, the portion of time left me I spent in draining, fencing and cultivating my lot.[365]

365. Watson, Manuscript History of Brigham Young.

Temporal Responsibilities of the Twelve

On July 9, 1841 Joseph visited Brigham Young in his log cabin in Nauvoo. His visit was not just to welcome him home or to thank him for his missionary labors in England. The purpose was to deliver to Brigham the word of the Lord:

> Dear and well-beloved brother, Brigham Young, verily thus saith the Lord unto you: My servant Brigham, it is no more required at your hand to

> leave your family as in times past, for your offering is acceptable to me.
>
> I have seen your labor and toil in journeyings for my name.
>
> I therefore command you to send my word abroad, and take especial care of your family from this time, henceforth and forever. Amen (D&C 126).

This was the second time the Prophet Joseph had received a revelation calling Brigham to stay home and to care for his family. The first was when he arrived in Far West in 1838 and now three years later, he was given the same message. The first kept Brigham from jumping into the fray of the Mormon War.

But Brigham was not sure of the reason for the second one. It was not, as might be surmised, for him to work on the temple. By summer of 1841, the temple foundation was finished and stones were being added to temple walls daily. Brigham would not know the answer until August 10, 1841, a little over a month after he and the other apostles had arrived back in Nauvoo.

Joseph called a meeting of the Twelve on that August date. At the meeting, he announced a sea change in their responsibilities. "The burthen of the business of the church in Nauvoo," said Joseph, "and especially as pertaining to the church lands, settling of the Saints after their arrival, and selling church lands" are now the responsibility of the Twelve.[366]

366. Watson, Manuscript History of Brigham Young, p. 106.

This marked a dramatic change from the role of the Twelve in Kirtland and Missouri. The assignment changed the earlier division of duties between standing high councils and the Twelve. The change meant that the Twelve would administer in Nauvoo just as they had among the branches abroad. The difference was Joseph Smith would be overseeing their work.

The shift in assignment underscored the importance of the Twelve in administration. From that August meeting forward, Joseph Smith spent months tutoring and mentoring the Twelve on how to administer the temporal affairs of the Church. There would be priesthood keys, even the "fulness of the priesthood that needed to be given for the Twelve to have the authority to preside over the Church and Kingdom of God," but that would come later. For now, the Twelve needed to be well-schooled on local administration.

On August 16, 1841 the Prophet Joseph Smith called a special conference of the Church. Brigham presided at the morning session and said:

> He hoped no one would view him and his brethren of the Twelve as aspiring, because they had come forward to take part in the proceedings. He could assure them that nothing could be farther from his wishes and those of the Twelve than to interfere with Church affairs in Zion and her stakes.
>
> He had been in the vineyard so long he had become attached to foreign missions, and nothing could induce him to retire therefrom and attend to the affairs of the Church at home but a sense of duty, the requirements of heaven, or the revelations of God.

The Prophet Joseph presided at the afternoon session. He spoke on the proper place of the Twelve in the Church. He wanted Latter-day Saints to understand that there had been an organizational realignment.

He explained that the Twelve would now work hand-in-hand with the First Presidency. In summary,

Joseph said:

> The time has come when the Twelve should be called upon to stand in their place next to the First Presidency, and attend to the settling of emigrants and the business of the Church at the stakes, and assist to bear off the kingdom victoriously to the nations.[367]

367. "An Epistle to the Twelve, to the Saints Scattered Abroad among the Nations," Times and Seasons 2 (September 1, 1841), pp. 521-522.

From the special conference on August 16, 1841 forward, Latter-day Saints became accustomed to not only being led by the Prophet Joseph and the First Presidency, but also by the Twelve. For example, on November 8, 1841 Brigham was the spokesman at the dedicatory service of the wooden baptismal font.

Afterwards, he was the first to be baptized for the dead in the font. In December 1841, Brigham "instruct[ed] the [temple] building committee in their duty" and promised them blessings from the Lord for their diligence.[368]

368. History, 1838-1856, volume C-1 [2 November 1838-31 July 1842], p. 1260.

None balked at his instructions or his role in the ceremonial dedication of the baptismal font for they knew, as president of the Twelve, Brigham stood next to the First Presidency.

Gospel Conversations

But for all the directions and instructions given by Brigham and others of the Twelve, it was still the Prophet Joseph Smith who was importuned to lead gospel conversations. "I could lean back and listen. Ah what pleasure this gave me," wrote Wandle Mace.

"[The Prophet] would unravel the scriptures and explain doctrine as no other man could. What had been mystery he made so plain it was no longer mystery."[369]

369. Wandle Mace Autobiography, pp. 101-102.

Brigham Young added, "[Joseph] took heaven, figuratively speaking, and brought it down to earth; and he took the earth, brought it up, and opened up, in plainness and simplicity, the things of God."[370]

370. Brigham Young, "Testimony of the Spirit—Revelation Given According to Requirements—Spiritual Warfare and Conquest, etc.," Journal of Discourses, 5:332.

During these gospel conversations, the Prophet Joseph spoke of the covenants and ordinances to be performed in the holy temple. He assured the Saints that by participating in temple ordinances, they would become more committed to a Christlike life and have a greater love for God.

He taught, "The pleasing joys of family ties and associations contribute to the happiness, power and dominion of those who attain to the celestial glory."[371] Wandle Mace wrote, "I ask, who understood anything about these things until Joseph being inspired from on high touched the key and unlocked the door of these mysteries of the kingdom."[372] Of these gospel conversations, Brigham said:

371. B. H. Roberts, Outlines of Ecclesiastical History (Salt Lake City: Deseret News, 1902), p. 394.

372. Wandle Mace Autobiography, pp. 101-102.

> I never did let an opportunity pass of getting with the Prophet Joseph and of hearing him speak in public or in private, so that I might draw understanding from the fountain from which he spoke, that I might have it and bring it forth when it was needed. . . .
>
> Such moments were more precious to me than all the wealth of the world.[373]

373. Brigham Young, "The Value of Attending Meetings—Gentile or Gentilism—Isolation—Preaching—Zion," Journal of Discourses, 12:269-270.

"No matter how great my poverty," Brigham said. "If I had to borrow meal to feed my wife and children, I never let an opportunity pass of learning what the Prophet had to impart."[374]

374. Brigham Young, "Plurality of Wives—The Free Agency of Man," Journal of Discourses, 3:266.

It was in private conversations with the Twelve that Joseph introduced and explained the law of plural marriage. Brigham Young wrote of his emotions upon learning the doctrine from Joseph:

> Some of these my brethren know what my feelings were at the time Joseph revealed the doctrine; I was not desirous of shrinking from any duty, nor of failing in the least to do as I was commanded, but it was the first time in my life that I had desired the grave, and I could hardly get over it for a long time. And when I saw a funeral, I felt to envy the corpse its situation, and to regret that I was not in the coffin, knowing the toil and labor that my body would have to undergo; and I have had to examine myself, from that day to this, and watch my faith, and carefully meditate, lest I should be found desiring the grave more than I ought to do...
>
> When I told Joseph what I understood, which was right in front of my house in the street, as he was shaking hands and leaving me, he turned round and looked me in the eyes, and says he—"Brother Brigham, are you speaking what you understand —are you in earnest?" Says I—"I speak just as the Spirit manifests to me." Says he—"God bless you, the Lord has opened your mind," and he turned and went off.[375]

375. Brigham Young, "Secret of Happiness—Self Examination—Joseph Smith a Man of Obedience to God—Baptism for the Dead—Temporal and Spiritual One—a Dream—Order of Enoch, the Order of God—A Good Word for the Women," Journal of Discourses, 18:241.

Clearly, Joseph was pleased that Brigham understood the doctrine and practice of plural marriage. Knowing that others would be slow to understand, Brigham and those who participated in the law of plural marriage were told to keep their actions confidential.

When confidences were broken, the practice proved the most challenging aspect of the Restoration. It became a trial of faith, as it violated cultural and legal norms. In Nauvoo, Joseph Smith married additional wives and authorized Brigham and a few other leading brethren to enter the practice also, with Joseph and Heber C. Kimball officiating.[376]

376. See Kate B. Carter, Brigham Young: His Wives and Family (Salt Lake City: Daughters of the Utah Pioneers, 1965).

An Endowment from God and a Blessing from a Prophet

Among the first to receive the sacred endowment was Brigham Young. On May 4, 1842 Joseph asked Brigham and eight other brethren to come to his Red Brick Store on Water Street to receive their endowment. In the upper story of that small store, Joseph introduced the brethren to "the ancient order of things for the first time in these last days."[377]

377. History, 1838-1856, volume C-1 [2 November 1838-31 July 1842], p. 1328.

They were given an endowment of ordinances necessary for them to return to the presence of the Lord and gain eternal exaltation.

In addition to an endowment, Brigham was privileged to receive a priesthood blessing at the hands of the Prophet Joseph Smith. On November 26, 1842 Joseph wrote, "Went to visit E[lde]r Brigham Young who was taken sick very suddenly."[378] Brigham wrote of his illness and of Joseph's tender care:

378. Journal, December 1841-December 1842, p. 210. Joseph Smith Papers.

> I was suddenly attacked with a slight fit of apoplexy. Next morning I felt quite comfortable; but in the evening at the same hour that I had the fit the day before, I was attacked with the most violent fever I ever experienced.
>
> The Prophet Joseph and Elder Willard Richards visited and administered unto me; the Prophet prophesied that I should live and recover from my sickness. He sat by me for six hours, and di-

rected my attendants what to do for me. In about thirty hours from the time of my being attacked by the fever, the skin began to peel from my body, and I was skinned all over.

I desired to be baptized in the river, but it was not until the 14th day that Brother Joseph would give his consent for me to be showered with cold water, when my fever began to break, and it left me on the 18th day, I laid upon my back, and was not turned upon my side for eighteen days...[379]

379. Brigham Young, "History of Brigham Young," Millennial Star (March 12, 1864), p. 167.

When the fever left me on the 18th day, I was bolstered up in my chair, but was so near gone that I could not close my eyes, which were set in my head—my chin dropped down and my breath stopped. My wife [Mary Ann], seeing my situation, threw some cold water in my face, that having no effect, she dashed a handful of strong camphor into my face and eyes, which I did not feel in the least, neither did I move a muscle. She then held my nostrils between her thumb and finger, and placing her mouth directly over mine, blew into my lungs until she filled them with air. This set my lungs in motion, and I again began to breathe.[380]

380. Watson, Manuscript History of Brigham Young, pp. 124-125.

That Brigham survived the effects of apoplexy, an incapacity resulting from a cerebral hemorrhage or stroke, to function at a full level again is a miracle. Before the miracle occurred, it took time, a baptism in the Mississippi, and the loving care of his wife and a prophet.

Joseph knew that Brigham must overcome apoplexy and lead the Church. To do so necessitated a full recovery.

The City on a Hill

By late fall of 1843, Latter-day Saints had tamed a swamp, reclaimed a wilderness, and built a progressive city from the flats to the bluffs. Craftsmen, artisans, and skilled laborers had created a legendary community that was spoken of with envy as the "Jewel of the Mississippi." Hyrum Smith believed that what he saw in houses, shops, and civic buildings was just the beginning for "we shall have the largest city in the world."[381]

381. "Conference Minutes," Times and Seasons (August 1, 1844), p. 598.

Although Nauvoo never came close to being the largest city in the world, with the number of immigrants added to the residents of Nauvoo in 1843, some claimed the city rivaled Chicago in population. Of the great gathering to Nauvoo, Brigham Young said:

> Who is the author of this work and gathering? Joseph Smith, the Prophet, as an instrument in the hands of God, is the author of it. He is the greatest man on earth.
>
> No other man, at this age of the world, has power to assemble such a great people from all the nations of the earth, with all their varied dispositions, and so assimilate and cement them together that they become subject to rule and order. This the Prophet Joseph is doing. He has already gathered a great people who willingly subject themselves to his counsel, because they know it is righteous.[382]

382. Watson, Manuscript History of Brigham Young, pp. 140-141.

With so many immigrants in town, a diverse social and ethnic interest found expression. Southerners brought refinement, Northerners introduced the Protestant work ethic, and British converts brought the hope that the status of "ladies and gentlemen" was possible for every man and woman in the city. As the diverse Saints carved their niche in Nauvoo's society, they sought cultural expression in music, theater, dance, parades, and the arts. For the "young at heart," a circus or a riverboat excursion opened a vista of cultural wonder, a window to the world.

A poet memorialized events and people of the vibrant city of Nauvoo:

> O tell me not of Ancient Rome,
> of Athens, or of Troy:
> Gone, gone is all their greatness
> without one gleam of joy,
> Nor speak ye yet more modern names,
> tho fair and lovely too;
> What is their beauty, what their fame,
> compared to fair Nauvoo?[383]

383. "Nauvoo," Times and Seasons (October 15, 1844), p. 687.

The Cultural Hall was the hub of Nauvoo's nightlife. The first stage play presented in the hall was Pizzaro, starring none other than Brigham Young. He once observed:

> If I were placed on a cannibal island and given a task of civilizing its people, I should straightway build a theatre... On the stage of a theatre can be represented in character evil and its consequences, good and its happy results and rewards, the weaknesses and follies of man and the magnanimity of the virtuous life.[384]

384. Charles Metten, "Drama," in Daniel H. Ludlow, ed., Encyclopedia of Mormonism 5 vols. (NY: Macmillan, 1992), 1:429.

For those wishing to pursue academics, classes were offered by professors Orson Pratt and Orson Spencer at the University of Nauvoo. A town lending library boasted 200 volumes on science, world religion, history, and literature. For the fundamental courses of reading, writing, and arithmetic, small schoolrooms welcomed students from the community.

For those who enjoyed clever quips, Brigham Young's lines provided a wry smile:

> To live with Saints in Heaven is bliss and glory,
> To live with Saints on Earth is another story.[385]

385. Richard Neitzel Holzapfel and Jeni Broberg Holzapfel, Women of Nauvoo (Salt Lake City: Bookcraft, 1992), p. 69.

The most unforgettable parties were hosted at the Mansion House. The party commemorating Joseph and Emma Smith's 15th wedding anniversary began at ten o'clock in the morning. "Conversation continued on various topics until two o'clock, when twenty one [friends] sat down to the dinner table, and Emma and myself waited on them," wrote Joseph.[386] The party didn't end until favorite songs were sung.

386. History 1838-1856, volume D-1 [1 August 1842-1 July 1843], p. 1455.

Few could deny that by fall of 1843, Nauvoo, with its temple walls rising and the city alive with industry and artistic expression, was on its way to becoming the prophesied "light of the world—a city set upon a hill."[387] Orchestrating the administrative growth, building, and the artistic expressions was the Prophet Joseph Smith with Brigham Young at his side.

387, Grant, in Conference Report, April 1900, 21.

Joseph Smith. Steel engraving from a sketch made by Frederick Piercy.

Chapter Eleven

A US Presidential Candidate Murdered

By November 1843, newspaper editors across the nation were posing the question, "Who will be the next President?" From New York to Michigan, the Carolinas and Missouri, the question begged for an answer in the united, but too often divided states.

Acting "in behalf of the Church of Jesus Christ of Latter-day Saints," Joseph Smith sent letters to five leading US presidential candidates—Martin Van Buren, Lewis Case, Henry Clay, John C. Calhoun, and Richard Johnson—asking, "What will be your rule of action relative to us as a people [the Latter-day Saints], should fortune favor your ascension to the chief magistracy?"[388]

388. Letter to John C. Calhoun, 4 November 1843, p. 1. Joseph Smith Papers.

Martin Van Buren and Richard Johnson did not reply to Joseph's query. The response of Democratic hopeful Lewis Case is not available for review. Henry Clay, the leading candidate of the Whig Party, penned:

> I can enter into no engagements, make no promises, give no pledge to any particular portion of the people of the United States. If I ever enter into that high office I must go into it free and unfettered, with no guarantees.[389]

389. "Correspondence between Gen. Joseph Smith and the Hon. Henry Clay," Times and Seasons 5, no. 11 (June 1, 1844), p. 544.

Southerner John C. Calhoun penned, "Candor compels me [to pen]... the case does not come within the jurisdiction of the Federal Government."[390]

390. Letter from John C. Calhoun, 2 December 1843, p. 1. Joseph Smith Papers.

Joseph Smith wrote of his contempt for the unfettered stance of Clay and the narrow view of presidential power ascribed by Calhoun: "I am surprised that a man or men in the highest stations of public life should have made up such a fragile 'view' of a case."[391]

391. Letter to John C. Calhoun, 2 January 1844, p. 1. Joseph Smith Papers.

Letters of Clay and Calhoon and Joseph's rebuttal were printed in the Times and Seasons and Nauvoo Neighbor. Newspaper editors as far away as Columbus, Georgia and New York City sat up and took note. The Columbus Enquirer printed, "The disciples of Joe undoubtedly hold the balance of power in Illinois."[392]

392. Columbus Enquirer, February 14, 1844, in Michael K. Winder, Presidents and Prophets: The Story of America's Presidents and the LDS Church (American Fork, UT: Covenant Communications, 2007), p. 67.

The New York Daily Tribune printed, "If the Whigs are beaten, it will be by the votes of Nauvoo."[393]

393. New York Daily Tribune, June 10, 1844, in Winder, Presidents and Prophets, p. 67.

Joseph Smith a Candidate for US President

On January 29, 1844 at the Joseph Smith Red Brick Store, Church leaders met to discuss "the proper course for this people to pursue in relation to the coming Presidential election." After much discussion, Willard Richards proposed "an independent electoral ticket, and that Joseph Smith be a candidate for the next Presidency."[394] Joseph accepted the nomination. To Brigham, a vote for Joseph was a vote for upholding the Constitution of the United States. Brigham was confident that as US President, Joseph would use the power of his office to shield the Saints from further atrocities.

394. History, 1838-1856, volume E-1 [1 July 1843-30 April 1844], p. 1869.

It was not until "General Smith's Views of the Powers and Policy of the Government of the United States" was written and signed on February 7, 1844, however, that Joseph Smith sounded like a candidate for president of the United States. In Views, Joseph stated that if elected president he would annex Texas and Oregon and establish a national bank. He would "pay every man a reasonable price for his slaves out of the surplus revenue arising from the sale of public lands, and from the deduction of pay from the members of Congress." He would "reduce Congress at least two-thirds," grant the US president "full power to send an army to suppress mobs," and "abolish the practice in the army and navy of trying men by court-martial for desertion."[395]

395. History, 1838–1856, volume E-1 [1 July 1843–30 April 1844], P. 1883.

Whether the potential voter liked his proposals or not, none could deny that Joseph sounded presidential when he said, "We have had Democratic Presidents, Whig Presidents, a pseudo-Democratic-Whig President, and now it is time to have a President of the United States."[396] This statement caught the attention of Thomas Sharp, editor of the Warsaw Signal, who became the nemesis and enemy of Joseph. Before copies of Views were put in circulation, Sharp attacked the very idea of the Mormon Prophet being a candidate for the highest office in the land:

396. See "For President, Gen. Joseph Smith, Nauvoo, Illinois," Nauvoo Neighbor 2, no. 2 (May 8, 1844), p. 2; see "Gen. Smith's Views on the Government and Policy of the U.S.," Times and Seasons 5, no. 10 (May 15, 1844), p. 528.

> Well, Joe is fairly in the field! He can't go for Clay nor Van Buren, because they can't trample down the constitution to go for him. All right, Joe; no doubt you will be elected! and, . . . you will "administer justice with an impartial hand, and magnify and dignify the office of chief magistrate of the land."
>
> Faugh! Is there a man in the nation but believes that Joe Smith is a man of sterling worth and integrity, and of enlarged views; "honorable, fearless, and energetic;" and that "there is not a man in the United States more competent to the task?" Bah! . . . So good bye, Joe! when we can't vote for anybody else, maybe we will vote for you. No! We would as soon vote for Old Nick![397]

397. "The Presidency," Warsaw Signal 119, no. 2 (February 21, 1844), p. 2.

Attempting to ignore Thomas Sharp, copies of Views were sent to President John Tyler, his cabinet, justices of the Supreme Court, members of Congress, newspaper editors, postmasters, and other prominent men in the nation. Forty-five newspaper editors in 22 states responded. The editor of the New York Herald wrote:

> We received on Thursday some very curious and important intelligence from Nauvoo the capitol of the new Mormon Empire... Joe Smith... has taken the field as a political agitator, determined to wield political influence and political votes.[398]

398. The Nauvoo Neighbor printed verbatim the New York Herald editorial—see "For President, Gen. Joseph Smith, Nauvoo, Illinois," Nauvoo Neighbor 1, no. 47 (March 20, 1844), p. 2.

As for Thomas Sharp, he printed, "Candidly, from a review of your pamphlet we have come to the conclusion, that you are a greater dunce than nature ever intended you to be, and that you have about as much knowledge in your cranium of the relative limits and structures of our Governmental policy, as there is essential moisture in a January corn stalk," concluding, "Joe can't be beat except by a jackass."[399]

399. "Joe Smith's Views of the Powers and Policy of the General Government," Warsaw Signal 122, no. 5 (March 13, 1844), p. 2; "A Touch of the Sublime," Warsaw Signal 123, no. 6 (March 20, 1844), p. 2.

Brigham Young spoke up in defense and praise of Joseph Smith:

> [Joseph Smith] is the greatest man on earth. No other man, at this age of the world, has power to assemble such a great people from all the nations of the earth, with all their varied dispositions, and so assimilate and cement them together that they become subject to rule and order.
>
> This the Prophet Joseph is doing. He has already gathered a great people who willingly subject themselves to his counsel, because they know it is righteous.[400]

400. Watson, Manuscript History of Brigham Young, p. 140.

The Last Charge of the Twelve

With talk of the US presidential election dominating the national scene, at least one candidate had more important things on his mind. Joseph Smith asked his brother Hyrum Smith and the Twelve to attend a March 1844 meeting. The meeting was of such significance that the Twelve, for the first time, were asked to sign a document verifying their attendance:

> We, the undersigned, do hereby solemnly, sincerely, and truly testify before God, Angels, and men, unto all people to whom this certificate may come, that we were present at a Council in the latter part of the Month of March last, held in the city of Nauvoo in the upper part of the brick building situate[d] upon Water Street, commonly known here as "Joseph's Store," in which Council Joseph Smith did preside; and the greater part of the Twelve Apostles were present.[401]

401. "Declaration of 12 Apostles, [C. A. October 1844]," in Holzapfel and Shupe, Images of a Mormon Prophet, p. 15.

The signed document included these words from Joseph Smith at the meeting:

> Brethren, the Lord bids me hasten the work in which we are engaged. . . . It may be that my enemies will kill me; and in case they should, and the keys and power which rest on me not be imparted to you, they will be lost from the Earth; but if I can only succeed in placing them upon your heads, then let me fall a victim to murderous hands if God will suffer it, and I can go with all pleasure and satisfaction, knowing that my work is done, and the foundation laid on which the Kingdom of God is to be reared in this dispensation of the

> fulness of times. Upon the shoulders of the Twelve must the responsibility of leading this church hence forth rest until you shall appoint others to succeed you.[402]

402. Ibid.

Each of the Twelve received under the hands of Joseph and Hyrum Smith a confirmation of their responsibility to lead the Church. After the confirmations, the Prophet Joseph paced back and forth. As he did so, he "threw back the collar of his coat upon his shoulders" and said:

> I roll the burthen and responsibility of leading this church off from my shoulders on to yours. Now, round up your shoulders and stand under it like men; for the Lord is going to let me rest a while.[403]

403. Ibid., pp. 15-16

404. Undated draft of the statement in Brigham Young Papers, in Arrington, Brigham Young, American Moses, p. 110.

Joseph was still pacing when he said, "Since I have rolled the burthen off from my shoulders I feel as light as a cork. I feel that I am free. I thank my God for this deliverance."[404] Parley P. Pratt wrote of Joseph also saying:

> I know not why; but for some reason I am constrained to hasten my preparations, and to confer upon the Twelve all the ordinances, keys, covenants, endowments, and sealing ordinances of the priesthood, and so set before them a pattern in all things pertaining to the sanctuary and the endowment therein...
>
> Having done this he rejoiced exceedingly; for, said he, the Lord is about to lay the burden on your shoulders and let me rest awhile; and if they kill me, continued he, the kingdom of God will roll

on, as I have now finished the work which was laid upon me, by committing to you all things for the building of the kingdom according to the heavenly vision, and the pattern shown me from heaven.[405]

405. "P. P. Pratt's Proclamation," Millennial Star 5 (March 1845), p. 151.

Electioneering Volunteers

With the "burthen" rolled off his shoulders onto the Twelve, Joseph Smith went forward with his bid for the US presidency. He encouraged electioneering volunteers to make preparations to go to their fields of labor. At first 244 men volunteered, but within weeks, their numbers swelled to 337. As to the plausibility of volunteers propelling Joseph to the White House, the Prophet believed it not only possible but a determined fact. He said, "There is oratory enough in the Church to carry me into the presidential chair the first slide."[406]

Before the volunteers left Nauvoo, they were advised by Willard Richards to "use all honorable means in our power to secure" the election of Joseph Smith, saying, "open your mouth wide, and God shall fill it. Cut your quill, and the ink shall flow freely."[407] Hyrum Smith advised, "Lift up your voices like thunder; there is power and influence enough among us to put in a President."[408] Brigham Young said, "Some will vote for him for the novelty of the thing, and some to see what a prophet will do at the head of government."[409] John Taylor admonished, "Tell the people who would be the best man, and the most able statesman; who could stand uncorrupted by bribes, and uninfluenced by power, other than the power of justice, and the cause of right."[410] And with that said, the missionaries departed from Nauvoo with cheers from well-wishers—"Joseph Smith, the next President of the United States!"[411]

The Twelve were not idle bystanders as the election-

406. History, 1838-1856, volume E-1 [1 July 1843-30 April 1844], p. 1870.

407. Ibid., p. 1903.

408. Ibid., p. 1996.

409. History, 1838-1856, volume F-1 [1 May 1844-8 August 1844], p. 284.

410. "Conference," Times and Seasons 5, no. 5 (March 1, 1844), p. 455.

411. Letter from Lyman Wight and Heber C. Kimball, 19-24 June 1844, p. 1. Joseph Smith Papers.

eering volunteers spread news of Joseph's candidacy throughout the nation. Nine went east with Brigham in May 1844. Only John Taylor and Willard Richards of the Twelve remained behind in Nauvoo.

Peace in Nauvoo Threatened

At the very time electioneering volunteers were stumping for Joseph, peace in Nauvoo was threatened. "War and extermination is inevitable!" Thomas Sharp, editor of the Warsaw Signal, wrote. He called for,

> CITIZENS [TO] ARISE, ONE AND ALL!!! Can you stand by, and suffer such INFERNAL DEVILS! To rob men of their property and RIGHTS, without avenging them. We have no time for comment; every man will make his own. LET IT BE MADE WITH POWDER AND BALL!!!

The inevitable target of the proposed extermination was US presidential candidate Joseph Smith. "Joe Smith is not safe out of Nauvoo," wrote Sharp in the Warsaw Signal. "We would not be surprised to hear of his death by violent means in a short time. He has deadly enemies... The feeling of this country is now lashed to its utmost pitch, and will break forth in fury upon the slightest provocation."[412] In spite of the publicized threat of murder, Joseph Smith was calm: "God Almighty is my shield, and what can man do if God is my friend?"[413]

Joseph's calm resolve was tested in June 1844. It began with the printing of the Nauvoo Expositor. The first and only issue of that newspaper charged Joseph with indulging in whoredoms and abusing political power. It branded him as a base seducer, liar, and murderer.

412. "Matters and Things at Nauvoo," Warsaw Signal, (May 29, 1844), p. 133.

413. History, 1838-1856, volume D-1 [1 August 1842-1 July 1843], p. 6 [addenda].

Joseph, acting as mayor of Nauvoo, met with the Nauvoo city council to discuss the libelous accusations printed in the Expositor. The official decision stemming from the discussions was to denounce the newspaper as a public nuisance and authorize the sheriff to stop future publications.

When the Nauvoo Expositor press and building were destroyed, the owners and proprietors of the Expositor seized the opportunity to bring charges against Joseph and his brother Hyrum. The Smith brothers were arrested and discharged twice for charges stemming from the destruction of the Nauvoo Expositor, but legal court proceedings did not pacify those who clamored for blood. Yet Joseph said, "I shall not be sacrificed until my time comes; then I shall be offered freely."[414]

414. Ibid.

Hyrum Smith was not as calm as his brother. After the destruction of the Nauvoo Expositor building and the subsequent court trials, he wrote to Brigham Young on June 17, 1844:

> There has been for several days a great excitement among the inhabitants in the adjoining Counties. Mass meetings are held upon mass meeting, drawing up resolutions to utterly exterminate the Saints. The excitement has been gotten up by the Laws, Fosters, and the Higbees; and they themselves have left the City and are engaged in the mob. They have sent their runners into the State of Missouri to excite them to murder and bloodshed, and the report is that a great many hundreds of them will come over to take an active part in murdering the saints. The excitement is very great indeed.
>
> It is thought best by [Brother Joseph and] myself, and others, for you to return without delay, and the

rest of the Twelve and all the Elders that have gone out from this place, and as many more good and faithful men as feel disposed to come up with them. Let wisdom be exercised, and whatever they do, do it without a noise. You know we are not frightened but think it best to be well prepared and be ready for the onset; and if it is extermination—extermination it is, of course.

Communicate to the others of the Twelve with as much speed as possible, with perfect stillness and calmness. A word to the wise is sufficient and a little powder, lead and a good Rifle can be packed in your luggage very easy without creating any suspicion.

There must be no excuses made, for wisdom says that a strict compliance with this request will be for our safety and welfare.

In haste, I remain yours in the firm bonds of the new and Everlasting Covenant.
—Hyrum Smith[415]

415. Letter to Brigham Young, 17-20 June 1844, June 17, 1844, pp. 1-2, Joseph Smith Papers.

Joseph was concerned with the sentiment and facts presented in the letter. He advised Hyrum not to send it. The letter was never sent.

Joseph and Hyrum in Carthage

The Prophet Joseph made an attempt to escape a martyr's fate. He and his brother Hyrum left Nauvoo at about two o'clock in the morning of June 23, 1844 and were rowed across the Mississippi River to the banks of Iowa. There they made plans to go west. Their plans were thwarted when ill-advised friends asked Joseph to accede to the law in Carthage.

Early on Monday morning June 24, 1844, the Prophet Joseph and his brother Hyrum began their last journey to Carthage. As Joseph paused to look over the beautiful city of Nauvoo that he had so carefully orchestrated, he said, "This is the loveliest place and the best people under the heavens; little do they know the trials that await them."[416] To friend Dan Jones he confessed:

> I love the city of Nauvoo too well to save my life at your expense. If I go not to them [Carthaginians], they will come and act out the horrid Missouri scenes in Nauvoo. I may prevent it. I fear not death. My work is well nigh done. Keep the faith and I will die for Nauvoo.[417]

For Joseph and Hyrum Smith, Carthage was a scene of broken promises, conspiracy oaths, illegal arraignment, and incarceration, "Could my brother Hyrum but be liberated," Joseph mused, "it would not matter so much about me."[418] To his wife Emma he confided, "I am very much resigned to my lot, knowing I am justified and have done the best that could be done. Give my love to the children and all my Friends."[419]

In the early afternoon of June 27, two members of the Twelve—John Taylor and Willard Richards—visited the Smith brothers in Carthage Jail. In the bedroom on the second floor of the jail, John Taylor was asked to sing a hymn that harmonized with their sentiments:

> In pris'n I saw him next, condemned
> To meet a traitor's doom at morn.
> The tide of lying tongues I stemmed,
> And honored him 'mid shame and scorn.
> My friendship's utmost zeal to try.

416. History, 1838-1856, volume F-1 [1 May 1844-8 August 1844], p. 151.

417. Dan Jones, "History of the Latter-day Saints, from their establishment in the year 1823, until the time that three hundred thousand of them were exiled from America because of their religion, in the year 1846," pp. 73-83, as published and translated from Welch in Ronald D. Dennis, trans., "The Martyrdom of Joseph Smith and His Brother Hyrum," BYU Studies 24, no. 1 (1984), p. 96.

418. History, 1838-1856, volume F-1 [1 May 1844-8 August 1844], p. 168.

419. Letter to Emma Smith, 27 June 1844, pp. 1-2. Joseph Smith Papers.

> He asked if I for him would die.
> The flesh was weak; my blood ran chill,
> But my free spirit cried, "I will."[420]

420. "A Poor Wayfaring Man of Grief," LDS Hymnal, p. 29.

Around five o'clock in the afternoon of June 27, "an armed mob—painted black—of from 150 to 200 persons" surrounded the jail. In spite of early attempts to defend themselves from lawless mob violence, the men could not stop the brutal assassins. Hyrum Smith was the first to fall from an assassin's bullet. He fell to the ground exclaiming, "I am a dead man!" Upon seeing him fall, Joseph sobbed, "Oh dear, brother Hyrum!"[421]

421. Historian's Office, Martyrdom Account, Draft, pp. 53-54. Joseph Smith Papers.

Joseph then stepped toward the bedroom window. As he did so, bullets shot from the doorway struck him as did two shots from outside. He fell from the window to the ground below exclaiming, "O Lord, My God!" (D&C 135:1).

Brigham learns of the Martyrdom

On June 27, 1844, the day Joseph and Hyrum Smith were martyred in Carthage, Brigham wrote, "Spent the day in Boston with brother Woodruff... In the evening, while sitting in the depot waiting [for the train to Salem], I felt a heavy depression of Spirit, and so melancholy I could not converse with any degree of pleasure.I could not assign my reasons for my peculiar feelings."[422]

422. Watson, Manuscript History of Brigham Young, p. 169.

By July 9, Brigham had read newspaper accounts of the assassination of Joseph and Hyrum Smith in Carthage but discounted them as sensational rumors.

On July 16, Brigham and Orson Pratt were visiting at the home of a Brother Bement in Peterboro, New Hampshire. There, in the quiet of the home, they listened as a letter was read giving details of the deaths of Joseph and Hyrum at Carthage.

Brigham recalled, "The first thing which I thought of was, whether Joseph had taken the keys of the kingdom with him from the earth... Bringing my hand down on my knee, I said 'the keys of the kingdom are right here with the Church.'"[423] On July 17, Brigham was in Boston with Wilford Woodruff, who penned:

423. Brigham Young, "History of Brigham Young," Millennial Star 26 (June 4, 1864), p. 359.

> Elder Brigham Young arrived in Boston this morning. I walked with him to 57 Temple Street, and called upon Sister Vose. Brother Young took the bed and gave vent to his feelings in tears. I took the big chair, and veiled my face, and for the first time gave vent to my grief and mourning for the Prophet.[424]

424. History, 1838-1856, volume F-1 [1 May 1844-8 August 1844], p. 273.

Although the void caused by the death of Joseph and Hyrum Smith would never be filled, Brigham and Wilford knew all was not lost even as they vented their sorrow in tears. Joseph was gone, but the keys for leading the Church were not. Wilford recorded:

> [Joseph Smith] told us that he was going away to leave us, going away to rest. Said he, "You have to round up your shoulders to bear up the kingdom. No matter what becomes of me, I have desired to see that Temple built, but I shall not live to see it. You will; you are called upon to bear... this kingdom." This language was plain enough, but we did not understand it any more than the disciples of Jesus when he told them he was going away, and that if he went not the Comforter would not come.[425]

425. Wilford Woodruff, "The Holy Ghost—Laboring in Faith—The Kingdom of God—Patriarchal Marriage," Journal of Discourses, 13:164.

While waiting in Boston for word from others of

the Twelve, Brigham received a letter from his wife Mary Ann confirming that Joseph and Hyrum Smith were dead:

> My Dear Companion... Our Dear Br. Joseph Smith and Hiram has fell victims to a verocious mob. The great God of the creation only knows whithe[r] the rest shall be preserved in safety or not. We are in tolerable good health at present. I have been blessed to keep my feelings quite calm through all the storm. I hope you will be careful on your way hom[e] and not expose yourself to those that will endanger your life. Yours in hast[e]. If we meet no more in this world may we meet where parting is no more. Farewell.[426]

426. Letter of Mary Ann Young to Brigham Young, June 30, 1844. Church History Library.

Brigham Young

Chapter Twelve
An Eternal Bond

The brethren waited a week in Boston for Lyman Wight to join them. They spent their time comforting the Saints in the area, assuring them that keys for leading the Church rest with the Twelve, and that Mormonism is not dead.

When Elder Wight arrived from Washington DC, the brethren left Boston and headed to Albany, New York, where they were joined by Orson Hyde. Making in all a traveling party of six—Brigham Young, Heber C. Kimball, Orson Pratt, Wilford Woodruff, Lyman Wight, and Orson Hyde—they now took a direct route to Nauvoo. Traveling by rail, stagecoach, and steamer they journeyed to Buffalo, Detroit, Chicago and Galena before arriving in Nauvoo at 8 p.m. on Tuesday, August 6, 1844.

It was not until Brigham listened to the words of loved ones that he fully comprehended the great sorrow that draped Nauvoo since the martyrdom of Joseph and Hyrum Smith. Shops were closed, hotel rooms were empty, and gardens went unattended. There was not even chatter on the streets. It was as if the very lifeblood of Nauvoo had been extinguished. The martyrdom had taken its toll.

Cheerful Saints, like Vilate Kimball, were still in tears. "I witnessed their tears, and groans [of the widows], which was enough to rent the heart of an adamant. Every brother and sister that witnessed the scene

427. Ronald K. Esplin, "Life in Nauvoo, June 1884: Vilate Kimball's Martyrdom Letters," BYU Studies 19 (Winter 1979), p. 238.

428. Newel Knight in William G. Hartley, "They are My Friends," A History of the Joseph Knight Family 1825-1850 (Provo UT: Grandin Book Company, 1986), pp. 153-154.

felt deeply to sympathize with them."[427]

Newel Knight wrote, "O how I loved those men, and rejoiced under their teachings! It seems as if all is gone, and as if my heart strings will break, and were it not for my beloved wife and dear children I feel as if I have nothing to live for."[428]

Nearly succumbing to the palpable sorrow of Nauvoo, Brigham staggered under the weight of his calling. Nauvoo without Joseph was little more than a despairing city on the banks of the Mississippi. Brigham wrote to his daughter Vilate in Massachusetts:

> It has been a time of mourning. The day that Joseph and Hyrum were brought in from Carthage to Nauvoo, it was judged by many, both in and out of the Church that there were more than five barrels of tears shed. I cannot bear to think anything about it.[429]

429. Brigham Young to Vilate Young, August 11, 1844. Brigham Young Papers.

Brigham knew sorrow was not the answer, for it was not appropriate to retreat or succumb to his overwhelming sense of loss, especially at a time when newspaper editors were announcing the end of Mormonism. The editor of the New York Herald quipped:

> The death of the modern mahomet [sic] will seal the fate of Mormonism. They cannot get another Joe Smith. The holy city must tumble into ruins, and the 'latter day saints' have indeed come to the latter day.[430]

430. New York Herald, July 8, 1844, in Susan Easton Black and Kim C. Averett, Nauvoo (Salt Lake City: Deseret Book, 1997), p. 68.

It was not just newspaper editors that mused about the end of Mormonism. The Saints tossed to and fro with uncertainty as to whether the Church was still an entity.

Within Brigham, there was a dogged determination to move forward the work of God. He knew his role.

He knew his charge and knew that he must not fail. Others of the Twelve felt the same. Orson Hyde was heard to prophesy, "Instead of the work dying, it will be like the mustard stock that was ripe, that a man undertook to throw out of his garden, and scattered seed all over it, and next year it was nothing but mustard. It will be so by shedding the blood of the prophets—it will make ten Saints where there is one now."[431]

431. History, 1838-1856, volume F-1 [1 May 1844-8 August 1844], p. 275.

Sidney Rigdon and the Twelve

A growing threat to their determination had to be addressed. It was not the threat of mob violence if the Saints continued in their faith. It was not the threat trumped up by Thomas Sharp of Warsaw that extermination was inevitable.

It was a threat from within. Sidney Rigdon, who had served in the First Presidency of the Church, had returned from Pittsburgh, Pennsylvania to Nauvoo. He told all who would listen that he was called to be the guardian of the Church and there would never be another like the Prophet Joseph who died holding the keys of the kingdom.

Rigdon claimed divine appointment to guard the faith. He lamented that the Saints would never finish the Nauvoo Temple and their work in Nauvoo was done. He told the Saints to be of good cheer, for Pittsburgh awaited them as did their Savior Jesus Christ.

The challenge of Sidney Rigdon to the leadership of the Twelve was not something to brush off or ignore. The Saints must know of Joseph's last charge to the Twelve and that the keys to lead the Church rested with the Twelve.

On August 7, 1844, the day after Brigham and the other five apostles arrived in Nauvoo they met at the home of John Taylor to discuss the issue of keys and succession. After discussing the false claims of Sidney Rigdon, the Twelve sent word throughout Nauvoo that a meeting of all high priests would be held that afternoon in the Seventies Hall on Parley Street.

During the meeting of near overflow capacity in the hall, Brigham called upon Sidney Rigdon to explain his claim to guardianship of the Church. Seemingly unmoved by the authority of the Twelve, Rigdon confidently stood before the assembly and told of a vision in which—

> It was shown to me that this Church must be built up to Joseph, and that all blessings we receive must come through him. I have been ordained a spokesman to Joseph, and I must come to Nauvoo and see that the church is governed in a proper manner.
>
> Joseph sustains the same relationship to this church as he has always done. No man can be the successor of Joseph... I have been consecrated a spokesman to Joseph, and I was commanded to speak for him.[432]

432. Ibid., pp. 295-296.

When Sidney Rigdon finished his elaborate perception of his new role and his right to the succession of leadership, Brigham stood and spoke of the charge given the Twelve by the Prophet Joseph Smith:

> I have the Keys and the means of obtaining the mind of God on the subject... Joseph conferred upon our heads all the keys and powers belonging to the apostleship which he himself held before he was taken away, and no man or set of men can get between Joseph and the Twelve in this world or the world to come.[433]

433. Ibid., p. 296.

The high priests had listened to conflicting views on succession. On the one hand, Rigdon professing guardianship, and on the other, Brigham professing the keys rest with the Twelve. The choice was theirs but no vote was called.

That same scene of conflicting views was presented to the Church at-large the next day, on Sunday, August 8, 1844. The Saints assembled in a grove in Nauvoo at 10 a.m. and again in the afternoon for Sabbath meetings. No doubt, they had come to worship. This worship service would be different than any other they had attended. "That was a day never to be forgotten," Helen Mar Whitney recalled. The number in attendance was so great that some in the grove were "obliged to stand, it being impossible for half of the congregation to be seated."

The weather being cold, windy, and rainy was unusual for the August day. But crowds and weather had nothing to do with Helen Mar Whitney's comment that "[this was] a day never to be forgotten."[434]

434. Helen Whitney, "Scenes in Nauvoo," Woman's Exponent 11 (1882), p. 130.

Sidney Rigdon was invited to present his view on succession. He began his remarks at a makeshift stand in front of the congregation. When the wind picked up, he went to the back of the congregation and climbed atop a wagon so the wind would carry his message and the Saints could better hear his voice.

The assembly turned around on their benches and faced the wagon to listen to Sidney. After speaking for about an hour and a half on his claim to guardianship of the Church, Sidney Rigdon sat down.

Brigham was the next speaker. George Romney said, I shall never forget in this world or in the world to come the scene as Brigham Young arose after Sidney Rigdon had used up an hour and a half delivering an eloquent discourse. When Brigham got up the mantle of Joseph Smith fell upon him. It was Joseph's voice; it was Joseph's appearance, and I testify to you, if I never again do so on this earth, in the presence of God and angels, that this is verily the truth. This is true—that the mantle of Joseph did fall upon Brigham Young and the people knew it.[435]

435. Bishop George Romney, typescript account of testimony by Mary R. Ross, in England, Brother Brigham, p. 75.

George Romney was not alone in his remembrance of the visual change wrought upon Brigham Young. Benjamin F. Johnson recalled that as soon as Brigham started to speak,

> I jumped upon my feet, for in every possible degree it was Joseph's voice, and his person, in look, attitude, dress and appearance was Joseph himself, personified; and I knew in a moment the spirit and mantle of Joseph was upon him...
>
> I saw in the transfiguration of Brigham Young, the tall, straight and portly form of the Prophet Joseph Smith, clothed in a sheen of light, covering him to his feet; and I heard the real and perfect voice of the Prophet, even to the whistle, as in years past caused by the loss of a tooth said to have been broken out by the mob at [Hiram].[436]

436. Johnson, My Life's Review, pp. 103-104.

Mary Winters recalled people standing "to get a better chance to hear and see. I and my little companion of the day, Julia Felshaw, being small of stature, stood upon the benches that we, too might behold the wonderful transformation."[437]

437. Mary Winters Autobiography, typescript, pp. 13-14. Church History Library.

Elizabeth Barlow said "When Brigham Young, the President of the Twelve, began speaking I saw a change come over him, saw him take on the form of Joseph Smith, and heard his voice change to that of the Prophet's."[438] Mary Ensign wrote,

> Sidney Rigdon was one candidate. I was at the meeting when he stood in his carriage and harangued the people nearly three hours. He thought it his place to lead the people. The Saints did not know what to do. It seemed as though everything was at a standstill...Brigham Young stepped to the stand. It seemed as though the Prophet was before us, and had been resurrected. People craned their necks to get a better view of him, he so resembled the Prophet in looks and speech. Surely the mantle of the Prophet had fallen on Brigham. I remember so well, what father said on our way home after the meeting. In speaking to a friend about the circumstances he said, "They need not hunt any farther, Brigham Young is the man."[439]

Helen Mar Whitney wrote:

> I can bear witness with hundreds of others who stood that day under the sound of Brigham's voice, of the wonderful and startling effect that it had upon us. If Joseph had risen from the dead and stood before them, it could hardly have made a deeper or more lasting impression. It was the very voice of Joseph himself. This was repeatedly spoken of by the Latter-day Saints.[440]

The "Mantle of Joseph" preceded the words uttered by Brigham Young, who now stood and said to the vast congregation,

> Attention all! . . . For the first time in my life, for the first time in your lives, for the first time in the

438. Pamela Emeline Smith Grant (as told by Pamela E. Barlow Thompson), "Biography of Elizabeth Haven Barlow." FamilySearch.

439. Mary Dunn Ensign Autobiography and Testimony. Dated 1908 and 1914. FamilySearch.

440. Helen Whitney, "Scenes in Nauvoo," Woman's Exponent 11 (1882), p. 130.

kingdom of God in the 19th century, without a Prophet at our head, do I step forth to act in my calling in connection with the Quorum of the Twelve, as Apostles of Jesus Christ unto this generation—Apostles whom God has called by revelation through the Prophet Joseph, who was ordained and anointed to bear off the keys of the kingdom of God in all the world.

This people have hitherto walked by sight and not by faith. You have had the Prophet in your midst. Do you all understand? You have walked by sight and without much pleading to the Lord to know whether things were right or not.

Heretofore you have had a Prophet as the mouth of the Lord to speak to you, but he has sealed his testimony with his blood, and now, for the first time, are you called to walk by faith, not by sight. . . .

There has been much said about President Rigdon being President of the Church, and leading the people, being the head, etc. Brother Rigdon has come 1,600 miles to tell you what he wants to do for you. If the people want President Rigdon to lead them they may have him; but I say unto you that the Quorum of the Twelve have the keys of the kingdom of God in all the world.

The Twelve are appointed by the finger of God. Here is Brigham, have his knees ever faltered? Have his lips ever quivered? Here is Heber and the rest of the Twelve, an independent body who have the keys of the priesthood—the keys of the kingdom of God to deliver to all the world: this is true, so help me

God. They stand next to Joseph, and are as the First Presidency of the Church.

> I do not know whether my enemies will take my life or not, and I do not care, for I want to be with the man I love [Joseph Smith]. . . .
>
> I tell you, in the name of the Lord that no man can put another between the Twelve and the Prophet Joseph. Why? Because Joseph was their file leader, and he has committed into their hands the keys of the kingdom in this last dispensation, for all the world; don't put a thread between the priesthood and God.
>
> I will ask, who has stood next to Joseph and Hyrum? I have, and I will stand next to him.[441]

441. "History of Joseph Smith," Millennial Star 25 (April 4, 1863), p. 216; "History of Joseph Smith," Millennial Star 25 (April 11, 1863), pp. 231-232.

As Brigham finished speaking, Sidney Rigdon asked William W. Phelps, the man who wrote the hymn "Praise to the Man," to speak in his behalf. Instead of addressing the claims of Sidney Rigdon, W. W. Phelps said, "If you want to do right, uphold the Twelve."[442] Brigham Young then arose and called for a vote: "I will ask you as quorums, Do you want Brother Rigdon to stand forward as your leader, your guide, your spokesman" or the Twelve?[443] The vote was taken by "holding up the right hand." The vote was unanimous. All were in agreement that the Twelve held the keys to preside over the Church.

442. Smith, History of the Church, 7:238.

443. "History of Joseph Smith," Millennial Star 25 (April 25, 1863), pp. 264.

A relieved and grateful Brigham Young wrote in his diary on August 8, 1844:

> This day is long to be remembered by me, it is the first time I have met with the Church at Nauvoo

> since Bro. Joseph and Hyrum were killed . . . after Br. Rigdon had made a long speech to the saints,...
>
> I arose and spoke to the people, my heart was swollen with compassion toward them and by the power of the Holy Ghost, even the spirit of the prophets I was enabled to comfort the hearts of the Saints. In the afternoon according to my request the people assembled by thousands. I laid before them the order of the church and the power of the Priesthood. After a long and laborious talk of about two hours in the open air with the wind blowing, the church was of one heart and one mind they wanted the Twelve to lead the church as Brother Joseph had done in his day.[444]

444. Brigham Young diary, August 8, 1844, in Young, Here is Brigham . . . , pp. 366-370.

Under the Leadership of the Twelve

As the Twelve took their rightful place as leaders of the Church, the city of Nauvoo quickly returned to its former vibrancy. Brigham said, "All things are now reviving up again... the spirit of Joseph is here."[445]

445. Brigham Young to Vilate Young, August 11, 1844. Brigham Young Papers.

Shops opened, mills ran, and industry was seen on every side. To Illinois governor Thomas Ford, "The murder of the Smiths, instead of putting an end to [Mormonism] only bound them together closer than ever, . . . [giving] them new confidence in their faith."[446] Brigham saw to it that the name of the city of Nauvoo was changed to "The City of Joseph." As a city named after the Prophet Joseph Smith, it grew in wealth and numbers as never before. Brigham wrote to his friend Wilford Woodruff:

446. Thomas Ford, A History of Illinois, from Its Commencement as a State in 1818 to 1847 (MI: University of Michigan, 1854), p. 357.

> It is almost impossible to find an empty house or a room to rent. The tithing is coming in from nearly

> all the branches, and business moves as busily around the temple as it does around a beehive in May. Every man seems determined to do all he can to roll on the work of the Temple as fast as possible,...
>
> There never was a more prosperous time, in general, amongst the saints, since the work commenced. Nauvoo, or, more properly, the "City of Joseph," looks like a paradise... Many strangers are pouring in to view the Temple and the city. They express their astonishment and surprise to see the rapid progress of the Temple.[447]

To continue building the temple extracted a heavy toll upon the Saints as envy and jealousy of near neighbors heightened. A guard of 400 men kept watch "night and day around the Temple," wrote Hosea Stout. "No stranger [was] allowed to come within the square of the Temple Lot."[448]

Completing the temple and protecting the builders was all important. "I do not go out of doors, and look at that house [temple]," wrote Heber C. Kimball, "but the prayer of my heart is 'O, Lord save this people, and help them to build thy house.'"[449]

The plan of Brigham and the Twelve was to have the temple completed and the Saints endowed before they went west. Brigham had sat for many hours conversing with Joseph Smith about the West and listening to the prophet say, "If I were only in the Rocky Mountains with a hundred faithful men, I would then be happy."[450]

Although preparations for the move west proved disruptive to the prosperity of the Saints in the City of Joseph, Brigham was as determined to fulfill Joseph's

447. George A. Smith to Wilford Woodruff, April 13, 1845. Church History Library.

448. Juanita Brooks, ed., On the Mormon Frontier: The Diary of Hosea Stout, 1844-1861 2 vols. (Salt Lake City: University of Utah Press, 1964), 1:64.

449. "Speech of Elder H. C. Kimball, Delivered June 1, 1845," Times and Seasons 6 (August 1, 1845), pp. 987-988.

450. Brigham Young, "Knowledge in this Life Limited—The Lord Will Waste Away the Wicked—People do not Live to obtain What They most Desire—Joseph desired to Go to the Rocky Mountains—More for Us than Against Us—Will Go to Jackson County from the West—Exhortations to Merchants, Speculators, &c," Journal of Discourses, 11:16.

prophecy as he was to complete the temple:

> [Joseph] prophesied that the Saints would continue to suffer much affliction and would be driven to the Rocky Mountains, many would apostatize, others would be put to death by our persecutors, or lose their lives in consequence of exposure or disease, and some of you will live to go and assist in making settlements and build cities and see the Saints become a mighty people in the midst of the Rocky Mountains.[451]

451. History, 1838-1856, volume D-1 [1 August 1842-1 July 1843], p. 1362.

By fall of 1845 nearly every family was engaged in making wagons. Blacksmith, carpenters and wheelwrights were on call day and night. From the shop to the parlor, every available space was used to assemble boxes and wheels.

The stark dichotomy, an oddity of grand proportions, was not lost on observers. On the one hand, it was a scene of unparalleled tenacity to finish the temple, and on the other, to build a sturdy box with wheels to transport a family to the unknown and unchartered regions of the Rockies.

Although the temple was not complete, from December 1845 to February 1846, over 5,500 Latter-day Saints received their endowment. It was then that Brigham announced:

> Brethren awake!—... Let every branch in the east, west, north, and south, be determined to flee out of Babylon, either by land or by sea... Judgment is at the door and it will be easier to go now, than to wait until it comes.[452]

452. Smith, History of the Church, 7:516.

On February 4, 1846 Charles Shumway was the first

Latter-day Saint to cross the Mississippi River on what became the famous Mormon pioneer trek. Brigham left Nauvoo on February 15, 1846. Others followed.

With the Saints' departure and the subsequent fury of mobs, the glory of the City of Joseph was quickly extinguished. The once proud and beautiful city became draped in blight and crumbling ruin.

Few remained to mourn her loss, for the Saints of God had abandoned hearth and home for the valleys of the Rocky Mountains. But none forgot her days of grandeur, days when Saints donated tithes to build the temple, and days when Joseph and Brigham administered in the city. But there was a sense of excitement and adventure as the Saints moved forward to the unknown, unchartered West.

The burden placed on the shoulders of Brigham was real and for a lesser man, impossible. He was to lead the Saints to the Rockies, a distance of over 1,300 miles. He prayed mightily to the Lord as thousands of Saints followed him to the Iowa wilderness.

Most were unprepared for the arduous journey ahead. Temporary encampments were set up from the banks of the Mississippi to the Missouri River. In the camps, Latter-day Saints made preparations to cross the barren plains to the Rockies. In their last encampment at Winter Quarters, Brigham dreamed of the Prophet Joseph. He recorded details of his dream:

> While sick and asleep about noonday of the 17th inst., I dreamed that I went to see Joseph. He looked perfectly natural, sitting with his feet on the lower round of his chair. I took hold of his right hand and kissed him many times, and said to him: "Why is it that we cannot be together as we used to be? You have been from us a long time, and we want

your society and I do not like to be separated from you."

Joseph rising from his chair and looking at me with his usual earnest, expressive and pleasing countenance replied, "It is all right."

I said, "I do not like to be away from you."

Joseph said, "It is all right; we cannot be together yet; we shall be by and by; but you will have to do without me a while, and then we shall be together again." . . .

Joseph stepped toward me, and looking very earnestly, yet pleasantly said, "Tell the people to be humble and faithful, and be sure to keep the spirit of the Lord and it will lead them right. . . .

"Be sure to tell the people to keep the Spirit of the Lord; and if they will, they will find themselves just as they were organized by our Father in Heaven before they came into the world.

Our Father in Heaven organized the human family, but they are all disorganized and in great confusion."

Joseph then showed me the pattern, how they were in the beginning. This I cannot describe, but I saw it, and saw where the Priesthood had been taken from the earth and how it must be joined together, so that there would be a perfect chain from Father Adam to his latest posterity.

Joseph again said, "Tell the people to be sure to keep

the Spirit of the Lord and follow it, and it will lead them just right."[453]

453. Watson, Manuscript History of Brigham Young, pp. 119-120.

For the next three decades, Brigham echoed the words of the Prophet Joseph by telling the Saints to "keep the Spirit of the Lord and follow it." As for himself, the Holy Spirit was his guide. He wrote:

> My testimony is positive. . . . I know that the sun shines, I know that I exist and have a being, and I testify that there is a God, and that Jesus Christ lives, and that he is the Savior of the world. Have you been to heaven and learned to the contrary? I know that Joseph Smith was a Prophet of God, and that he had many revelations. . . . What I know concerning God, concerning the earth, concerning government, I have received from the heavens, not alone through my natural ability, and I give God the glory and the praise.[454]

454. Brigham Young, "Unbelief—The Saints require Constant Instruction—Contrast Between the Gospel of Christ and the Religions of Men—Evil would Cease among the Saints If They would Live their Religion—Gathering the Poor—Tithing—Knowledge of God—Progress of the Work is Due to the Operations of the Spirit," Journal of Discourses, 16:46.

On August 29, 1877 the last day of his mortality, Brigham was placed before an open window in the Lion House. "When he was placed upon the bed in front of the window he... open[ed] his eyes, he gazed upward, exclaiming: 'Joseph! Joseph! Joseph!'"[455]

The name of Joseph was the last word he uttered. No wonder, for it was said of Brigham:

455. Gates, The Life Story of Brigham Young, pp. 361-363.

> During the thirty three years that he has presided over the Church, since the martyrdom of the Prophet Joseph, his knees have never trembled, his hands have never shook; he has never faltered or quailed.
>
> However threatening the surroundings or prospects may have been, he has never been dismayed... The

> time will yet come when his presidency over The Church of Jesus Christ of Latter-day Saints will be pointed to as an epoch of wonderful events.[456]

In life Brigham had been separated from the Prophet Joseph Smith for 33 years. In death, they were united. Brigham had known that would be so, and he advised that at his interment there should be "no crying or mourning with anyone as I have done my work faithfully and in good faith."[457]

456. James R. Clark, comp., Messages of the First Presidency of The Church of Jesus Christ of Latter-day Saints 6 vols. (Salt Lake City: Deseret Book Co., 1965-1975), 2:298.

457. Arrington, Brigham Young, American Moses, p. 399.